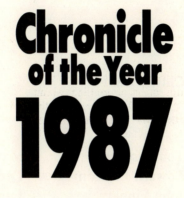

Chronicle
of the Year
1987

Chronicle of the Year 1987

Has been conceived and published by Jacques Legrand

Editor in Chief:	Clifton Daniel
Executive Editor:	John W. Kirshon

Correspondents:

Tom Anderson	Marjorie Hunter
Edward Edelson	Drew Middleton
John Finney	James Tuite

Staff Writers: Bob Blum, Susan Breen, Kevin Delaney, Philip Farber, James Forsht, John Goolrick, Catherine Hulbert, Louis M. Nevin Jr., Tod Olson, Roberta Oster, Karen Rohan, Marianne Ruuth, Steven T. Taylor, Pascale Thumerelle

Editorial Research: Tod Olson *(Editor)*
Kristie Simco

Photo Research: Steven T. Taylor *(Editor)*
Veronique de Saint Andre *(SIPA)*

EDP: Catherine Balouet *(Manager)*
Dominique Klutz *(Software Engineer)*
Darin Hamilton *(DPC)*

Production: Maxine Lee Fatt *(Manager)*
Tanya Rahl Nádas
Rose Ann Caris

Marketing: Peter J. Clark *(Director)*

ISBN 0-942191-04-8
Typesetting: Digital Prepress Center (DPC), Yonkers, N.Y.
Printing & Binding: Brepols, Turnhout, Belgium

Chronicle
of the Year
1987

Chronicle

Publications

Mount Kisco, N.Y.

Su	Mo	Tu	We	Th	Fr	Sa
				1	2	3
4	5	6	7	8	9	10
11	12	13	14	15	16	17
18	19	20	21	22	23	24
25	26	27	28	29	30	31

1. Pasadena: Arizona State over Michigan 22-15 in Rose Bowl.

1. Peking: Students stage largest protest since 1976 (→ 5).

1. U.S.: Florida now fifth in population, behind California, New York, Texas, Pennsylvania.

3. Washington: Frank C. Carlucci sworn in as national security adviser (→ 8).

3. Abidjan, Ivory Coast: Brazilian jetliner crashes; 49 dead.

3. U.S. Dept. of Education study praises links between schooling and job market in Japan (→ 10).

4. Washington: Four noncancerous polyps removed from President Reagan's colon.

4. U.S.: Bank failures reported up 20% in 1986 (→ 8).

4. Sao Paulo, Brazil: Pele returns to soccer field first time in ten years in World Cup for Seniors.

4. Port Elizabeth, South Africa: Mixed-race Cabinet Minister Allan Hendrickse leads blacks onto whites-only beach (→ 8).

5. Washington: Reagan submits $102 bil. budget asking 3% hike in arms, curbs on farm aid, student loans, Medicare, Medicaid.

5. Moscow: Soviets reveal tax breaks to draw foreign firms into joint ventures in U.S.S.R. (→ 29).

6. Nicaragua: Civil war intensifying; 2,000 contras have crossed border from Honduras (→ 9).

6. Vietnam reports killing 500 in clash with Chinese troops.

7. U.S. requests FBI inquiry into burglary at International Center for Development Policy, one of 35 break-ins at offices of groups opposed to U.S. Central American policy.

8. Lincoln: Nebraska inaugurates Kay A. Orr, nation's first Republican woman governor.

8. Dakar: Secretary of State Shultz begins African tour, calling for extension of free market (→ 15).

8. Florida: Second contra group beginning training with U.S. military at secret location (→ 9).

9. Managua: New constitution put into effect; demonstrations test expansion of rights (→ 28).

Dow Jones index tops 2,000 first time

Flurry of activity on the floor.

Jan 8. The floor of the New York Stock Exchange looked like a New Year's celebration this afternoon. Traders threw paper into the air like confetti as the final bell sounded and the Dow Jones industrial average catapulted above the 2,000 mark. This has never happened before, and some financial analysts are so bullish that they predict 3,000 could be next.

The Dow index actually rose only eight points today, and some players on Wall Street were shaky and nervous. They are concerned that the economy is too sluggish to support the galloping market. Profit-takers also tangled with the bulls as they cashed in on the market's recent advances. But nobody could stop the momentum. In five days, the Dow has gone up five percent.

That is an enticing profit for small investors, who are fed up with measly returns of six percent on their certificates of deposit. Low inflation is also helping the market. And the weaker dollar is still attracting a stream of foreign capital into the United States (→ 14).

Congress to investigate Iran-contra deals

Jan 9. As the first item of business in the new, Democratic-controlled Congress, the House and Senate have established special panels to investigate the Iran-contra affair. Congressional leaders say the investigation should be carried out in a nonpartisan way.

The secret sale of arms to Iran and diversion of profits to the Nicaraguan rebels had been investigated by the Senate Intelligence Committee. Out of that inquiry leaked information linking Lieut. Col. Oliver L. North, a member of the National Security Council staff, to arms shipments to the contras. Caught up in a political firestorm, the White House made public documents designed to show the arms sales were intended to promote a more moderate regime in Iran. They also showed release of hostages was a consideration (→ 12).

Arson blamed for San Juan fire; 96 killed

Jan 4. Puerto Rico's Secretary of Justice, Hector Rivera Cruz, said today that the New Year's Eve blaze at the Dupont Plaza hotel "was a malicious fire, it was arson."

Rescue helicopters circle the hotel.

He indicated that authorities are investigating "people related to hotel operations." Officials now believe that a chemical substance, possibly a Molotov cocktail, may have ignited the fire. The number of deaths has risen to 96, making it the worst hotel fire in the United States in 40 years.

The Dupont Plaza was in the middle of a labor-management dispute and had been the target of threatening phone calls and three small fires in the two weeks that preceded the New Year's Eve catastrophe. A bomb threat two hours before the blaze was ignored by police after hotel officials assured them "there was no problem" (→ 13).

New galaxy sighted incredibly far away

Jan 6. Astronomers at the University of California say they have caught the first glimpse of the birth pangs of a giant galaxy containing a billion stars. Instruments pointed at an object designated radio wave source 3C 326.1, 12 billion light years from earth, have found "the first evidence of a massive galaxy seen during its formation stages long ago and far away," astronomer Hyron Spinrad told the American Astronomical Society's annual meeting. Radio and optical telescopes find 3C 326.1 to be a cloud of electrically charged hydrogen gas three times bigger than the Milky Way. Stars are being born as the cloud collapses in the process of forming a galaxy. The proto-galaxy is emitting a vast amount of radio wave energy as it evolves into a full-fledged galaxy.

African nationalists mark 75th birthday

Jan 8. Today is the birthday of the African National Congress, in the forefront of the struggle for equality in South Africa for 75 years. The outlawed group's leader, Nelson Mandela, is in jail. Its current President, Oliver Tambo, says he won't relinquish violence to free the country. The latest blow against apartheid was struck on the 4th, when the Rev. Allan Hendrickse led 150 blacks onto a whites-only beach in Port Elizabeth (→ 22).

Protester holds a poster of Mandela.

Chinese students demand free expression

Students make a bonfire of newspapers they said misrepresent their movement.

Jan 5. Mounting demonstrations by tens of thousands of college students in 11 Chinese cities came to a climax today when 500 Peking University students built a bonfire and burned copies of the Peking Daily to protest what they called distorted reporting. "Peking Daily, Go to Hell," read one banner hanging from a dormitory. The journal has denounced students' appeals for free expression, and it has ac-cused them of provoking anarchy.

The largest demonstration since the end of the Cultural Revolution in 1976 occurred on New Year's Day, when thousands of students defied a government ban and converged on Tien An Men Square in Peking. They sang the "Internationale," called for the public election of officials and urged support for the modernization program of China's leader, Deng Hsiao-ping (→ 12).

Family farm depression worst in 50 years

Jan 3. On a small farm in northern Iowa, tears welled in the eyes of a young mother as she told a visitor how hard life had become on the family farm. The woman, who asked not to be identified, said she

The small farm: a vanishing breed.

and her husband work 16 hours a day, seven days a week. They produce enough food to eat, but they make barely enough money to keep creditors away. The budget for their family of four is $9,000 a year.

This family is not alone. While huge fortunes are being made on Wall Street, the nation's farmers are suffering through their worst times in half a century. The number of farms dropped nine percent in the decade ending in 1985, and the younger generation sees the writing on the wall. The average farmer is getting older, and his children are fleeing to the cities.

The more farmers produce, the worse off many of them become. They are rewarded by the government to increase production, but higher supplies only force prices down. While much of the country continued to enjoy the Reagan era's prosperity last year, farm prices fell more than five percent (→ 3/2).

Japan challenging U.S. computer chips

Jan 5. Fearful that they are falling behind their Japanese competitors, American semiconductor manufacturers are planning to form a consortium to develop advanced technology. The effort is supported by the Defense Department, which worries that the decline of the U.S. semiconductor industry will leave it dependent on foreign suppliers for the silicon chips needed for advanced telecommunications and computer equipment. Recent reports by the Defense Department and Central Intelligence Agency said American chip makers were in danger of losing their technological lead in all but a small segment of the semiconductor market (→ 23).

Cardinal under fire after Mideast trip

Jan 10. According to a nine-paragraph statement issued jointly by virtually every major Jewish organization in the United States, John Cardinal O'Connor's recent trip to Israel "did more harm than good." O'Connor's trip came about in large part because of lobbying efforts by the same Jewish groups, who had originally hoped that the visit would forge a new bond between Israel and the Vatican, but many issues remain unresolved.

Americans losing mathematical race

Jan 10. New evidence ranks the mathematical ability of American primary and high school students among the lowest of any industrialized country. Attributable causes cited by researchers are repetitious curricula, less importance placed on mathematics in relation to other subjects, and the practice of placing students in classes by ability. Low expectations become self-fulfilling prophesies. In Japan, hard work is emphasized. In America, more importance is given to native ability. In Japan, school mobilizes the family, while American parents reportedly tend to stimulate a small child and then let the school take over (→ 19).

Why do snowflakes all differ in shape?

Jan 5. Though generations of poets have contemplated the uniqueness of each snowflake, science has only recently begun to tackle the enigma. Using complex computer models that combine new mathematical theories on random pattern formation with data on weather changes, scientists are predicting the shape a given crystal will take. The study may seem abstract, but it could have practical applications, such as in metallurgy.

Jan 4. Fifteen bodies have been dug out of a N.Y.-bound Amtrak train that hit three Conrail engines near Baltimore. Over 160 were hurt (→ 14).

Su	Mo	Tu	We	Th	Fr	Sa
				1	2	3
4	5	6	7	8	9	10
11	12	13	14	15	16	17
18	19	20	21	22	23	24
25	26	27	28	29	30	31

11. Washington: U.S. reportedly gave Iran and Iraq conflicting intelligence data to foster stalemate in Gulf war (→ 17).

12. Washington: Ex-national security adviser Robert McFarlane gives first indication Saudis gave contras $20 million (→ 17).

12. Peking: Chinese dismiss two university professors accused of aiding student protests (→ 16).

12. New York: Oil closes above $19 per barrel first time since Jan. 31, 1986 (→ 2/25).

13. Washington: Supreme Court upholds right to require leaves for pregnant women (→ 3/3).

13. New York: Eight of Mafia's "board of directors" get 40- to 100-year sentences (→ 3/2).

13. San Juan, Puerto Rico: Hotel worker indicted in Dupont Plaza hotel fire (→ 6/22).

13. Rome: Polish leader Gen. Wociech Jaruzelski meets with pope; no advance on opening of diplomatic ties (→ 2/19).

13. Frankfurt: Lebanese Muhammed Ali Hamadei arrested as pro-Iran terrorist (→ 6/24).

13. U.S.: AT&T bars pregnant women from making microchips to avoid risk of miscarriage.

14. Washington: Traces of marijuana found in Amtrak operators involved in rail accident (→ 5/4).

15. Washington: Shultz returns from African trip under fire for praising Liberian human rights.

15. Detroit: Audi recalls 250,000 cars for sudden accelerations.

16. New York: "Les Miserables" shatters Broadway records with $6.72 mil. in sales, five weeks before opening night (→ 3/12).

16. Bogota: Colombian media circulate protest warning country is dominated by drug traffickers (→ 2/5).

17. Iraqis claim bombing of Khomeini's home in Tehran, "capital of snakes and charlatans" (→ 2/9).

17. Virginia Beach: Shirley MacLaine begins ten-city tour of spiritual seminars—$300 per person: "$100 for mind, $100 for body, $100 for spirit."

Student protests oust Chinese party chief

Zhao, new party chief in China.

Jan 16. Following six weeks of student demonstrations for democracy in China, Hu Yao-bang, leader of the world's largest Communist Party, has been forced to resign.

Accused of making "mistakes on major political principles," Hu will be replaced, at least temporarily, by Prime Minister Zhao Ziyang as acting General Secretary of the party.

The move has been called a victory for conservatives, who have denounced the students as sympathetic to "bourgeois liberalism," a term of opprobrium reserved for Western ideas. The hard-liners apparently put pressure on Deng Hsiao-ping, China's leader, to dismiss Hu because he could not end the protests. Hu and Zhao, a consummate bureaucrat, have each been called Deng's likely successor.

Hu's ouster, according to observers, raises the question of whether China can attain the level of economic growth that has transformed other Asian nations (→ 3/2).

Afghanistan cease-fire efforts fail again

Jan 17. Despite government claims that all fighting has stopped, Western diplomats report that the seven-year-old conflict in Afghanistan is continuing.

Tens of thousands of guerrillas, chanting "Death to the Russians," assembled at Peshawar just over the border in Pakistan today. Leaders of the guerrillas, called mujahedeen, formally rejected the cease-fire declared by the Soviet-backed Afghan regime and announced plans to form their own government-in-exile. The truce and the government's offer of reconciliation were denounced as tricks to legitimize the Soviet Union's control of Afghanistan.

Recent visits to Kabul by senior Soviet officials reflect Moscow's growing eagerness to reduce its involvement in the country for both military and political reasons. But the Russians are unlikely to leave until the military situation stabilizes. There is no sign of that. The guerrillas, increasingly armed with American and other Western weapons, limit Soviet forces to the major cities and roads. The countryside belongs to them (→ 3/24).

Tradition meets technology: Mujahedeen (Islamic warrior) holds his ground.

Paley is called back in turnover at CBS

Jan 14. The CBS board of directors, trying to put some polish on the tarnished "Tiffany network," have voted unanimously to elect founder William S. Paley Chairman. Laurence Tisch was named President and Chief Executive. Last fall, the two ousted Thomas Wyman from the chairman's office.

It will take all of Paley's magic to rebuild the network. Morale has foundered since Tisch bought his way onto the board by purchasing nearly 25% of the stock. Making no secret of his desire to increase profits, Tisch masterminded the layoffs of at least 1,000 employees. One book division has been sold, and Tisch favors selling the highly profitable CBS Records group (→ 2/5).

Under-30's divorce at twice normal rate

Jan 12. Many see divorce as a mid-life phenomenon, but more marriages dissolve under age 30 than at any other time. In fact, the divorce rate for young couples more than doubles the national average. It increased 38 percent from 1970-1984. Unrealistic ideas of marriage, including emphasis on "fantastic sex," confusing sex with intimacy, and poor communication skills are cited as reasons. Also, many too young to marry do so because of premarital pregnancies.

Shawn replaced as New Yorker Editor

Jan 12. Robert A. Gottlieb, President and Editor-in-Chief of Alfred A. Knopf, was named Editor of The New Yorker magazine today, succeeding 79-year-old William Shawn, who has been the magazine's Editor for the past 35 years. Shawn's departure came as a shock to many staffers, some of whom believe an outsider will have a tough time running the magazine. Gottlieb's informal style contrasts with Shawn's legendary formality, but the two appear to have similar literary tastes. Gottlieb, 55, has edited many literary greats.

Americans divided over coloring old films

Laurel and Hardy in the modern era: before and after colorization.

Jan 12. "Criminal mutilation," says Woody Allen. "Sheer stupidity," thunders John Huston. "Artistic desecration," comments Directors Guild of America. The debate rages on: To color or not to color old black-and-white movies.

The colorizers answer that the original print is unmolested and admit they only want to make money. "People like color," they add. They compare coloring to dubbing dialogue for foreign audiences. "This is visual dubbing," they say. Some point to the reels of junk Hollywood turns out, the multiple sequels to "Friday the 13th" for instance. "Since when is taste the yardstick? And will coloring necessarily turn art into junk?" they ask. "Will they color Michelangelo's drawings next?" opponents retort.

West Bank Arabs battle Israeli troops

Jan 11. Acts of violence by Palestinian students continue to plague the Israeli-occupied West Bank. The bloodiest occurred recently near Jerusalem when students stoned Israeli troops. The troops fired on the students, killing two, and stone-throwing erupted at West Bank schools for another week. These acts lack political motivation but are rather revenge enacted by a frustrated generation of Palestinians who have known nothing but Israeli occupation. "We want any means of getting back at the Jews," one said, adding that PLO leader Yasser Arafat remains for the students "the symbol of the Palestinians. He is the stone we throw against the world."

Dollar driven down by American policy

Jan 14. The dollar dropped to a new low against the yen today as the White House gave renewed signals that it would not intervene to stop the decline. The dollar also reached a six-year low against the West German mark.

The decline of the dollar is a calculated tactic by the administration to reduce the U.S. trade deficit, which rose to $175 billion last year. By making the dollar cheaper, the government hopes to help American manufacturers sell more products abroad while discouraging imports from Japan and Europe. But many economists see a risk that an uninterrupted plunge of the dollar could disrupt international trade, bringing on a world recession (→ 19).

Saudis give $20 million in aid to contras

Jan 17. Saudi Arabia, at American request, contributed $20 million in support of the rebel forces in Nicaragua, congressional investigators disclosed today. Robert C. McFarlane, former national security adviser, told congressional investigators the Saudi aid was intended to buy nonlethal material for the contras at a time when Congress had cut off assistance to them. The disclosure brought to $40 million the amount the administration arranged for support of the contras, including a $10 million contribution from Brunei that the State Department says cannot be traced and $10 to $30 million that Attorney General Meese has estimated was diverted from arms sales to Iran.

The fund-raising and diversion present a question, being pressed by congressional investigators, as to whether the Reagan administration circumvented a series of laws passed by Congress, starting in 1984, restricting or banning aid to the contras. From the administration's standpoint, the laws were ambiguous in their application, providing such loopholes as raising money from foreign countries (→ 19)

"Today," tops on TV, is 35 years old

Jan 13. Celebrating its 35th anniversary, the "Today" show is first in the morning ratings, due largely to co-anchor Bryant Gumbel, 37. The former sportscaster was rated best interviewer by the Washington Journalism Review. Often labeled arrogant, Gumbel remembers when ratings were low and he was "booed with regularity." With the February departure of ABC's "Good Morning America" host David Hartman, Gumbel will be the undisputed leading man.

Homosexuals win child custody cases

Jan 17. Will a child raised by a homosexual parent become homosexual? Most homosexuals were raised by heterosexual parents and did not follow suit, some argue. Appellate and trial courts in many states have ruled that sexual orientation is not a factor in choosing a custodial parent, unless it can be demonstrated to be harmful to the child. A recent argument to get a child away from a homosexual ex-spouse cites increased risk of exposure to AIDS.

A wide array of enthusiasts are in New York this week to mark the centenary of Sherlock Holmes.

"Crime and Punishment," directed by Soviet exile Yuri Lyubimov, is now playing in Washington.

Blacks say Reagan policies hurt them

Jan 14. A leading civil rights group condemned the Reagan administration today, charging it used "morally unjust" and "economically unfair" policies to hurt American blacks. The National Urban League cited government statistics to show that blacks are falling further behind whites, economically and socially; that black unemployment and poverty are increasing; and that enforcement of civil rights laws is declining. League President John E. Jacob said blacks in the United States are "besieged by the resurgence of raw racism, persistent economic depression and the continued erosion of past gains" (→ 19).

Bearing the brunt of economic woes.

Su	Mo	Tu	We	Th	Fr	Sa
				1	2	3
4	5	6	7	8	9	10
11	12	13	14	15	16	17
18	19	20	21	22	23	24
25	26	27	28	29	30	31

18. Pittsburgh: United Steelworkers take pay and job cuts in new pact with USX (→ 30).

18. Ann Arbor, Mich.: Student bookstore closes, putting 75 members of Intl. Workers of the World out of work.

19. Montgomery: Guy Hunt replaces George Wallace as governor; sworn in with same Bible used for Jefferson Davis.

19. Washington: Officials reveal U.S. flight crews taking arms to contras were caught smuggling drugs (→ 23).

19. U.S.: American Heart Assn. says death rate from heart disease dropped 40% in 20 years.

20. Washington: Labor Dept. aide Joseph Cooper resigns, saying admin. pays "lip service" to equal opportunity laws (→ 21).

20. Seoul: Interior minister and national police chief ousted in torture death of student protester Park Chong Chol (→ 30).

20. U.S.: IBM earnings down 48.2% in fourth quarter (→ 21).

21. Washington: Atty. Gen. Edwin Meese backs plan to repeal Miranda Rights.

21. N.Y.: Dow drops first time since Jan. 1, despite 1.1% inflation rate reported today (→ 2/1).

22. U.S.: A.N.C. chief Oliver Tambo defends use of violence against S. African whites (→ 28).

22. Manila: 18 die as police open fire on leftist protesters (→ 29).

23. Salt Lake City: Mark Hoffman, dealer in Mormon documents, pleads guilty to murder of two; father asks execution.

23. Washington: Sen. Moynihan proposes complete overhaul of welfare system (→ 3/29).

23. Tokyo: Japan drops requirement limiting arms spending to 1% of G.N.P. (→ 27).

24. U.S.: Poll gives Bush (36%) and Hart (33%) clear leads for 1988 nominations (→ 2/19).

24. Melbourne: Hana Mandlikova breaks Martina Navratilova's 58-match win streak to take Australian Open 7-5, 7-6.

24. Beirut: Gunmen in police uniforms seize three U.S. teachers at Beirut University (→ 28).

Rights march, biggest since 60's, harassed

Jan. 24. As Ku Klux Klansmen and their sympathizers jeered and chanted "Nigger, go home," tens of thousands of civil rights supporters marched through the little town of Cumming, Georgia, today, guarded by an army of National Guardsmen and law enforcement officials. It was one of the largest civil rights demonstrations since a 1965 rally held after the Rev. Dr. Martin Luther King led a march from Selma to Montgomery, Alabama.

Forsyth County, scene of today's march, has been an almost totally white stronghold since blacks were driven out earlier this century after the rape and subsequent death of a white woman said to have been attacked by three black men.

Among those in today's march were Mrs. Coretta Scott King, the widow of Dr. King; Atlanta Mayor

A Confederate flag greets marchers.

Andrew Young; and two likely contenders for the Democratic nomination for President, Sen. Gary Hart and the Rev. Jesse Jackson (→ 25).

Contra suppliers reported smuggling drugs

Jan. 23. A new wrinkle has been added to the Iran-contra affair by the disclosure that American air crews covertly flying supplies to the contras may have smuggled drugs on their return flights to the United States. Federal drug investigators were said to have uncovered evidence of such drug smuggling by the covert air supply operation set up by Lieut. Col. Oliver L. North. There was no evidence, however, that Colonel North knew of any

drug smuggling or that it was conducted to help the contras.

Meanwhile, a staff report prepared while Republicans controlled the Senate Intelligence Committee criticized the administration's arms sales to Iran but said there was no evidence President Reagan knew of diversion of profits from the sales to the Nicaraguan insurgents. Vice President Bush expressed confidence the Iran-contra affair was "under control" (→ 29).

Roll out the barrel: Polka still thrives

There is a Polka Belt in America, divided into ethnic styles. From New England and across the land are heard brassy Czech polkas, Tex-Mex polkas, oompah-style German polkas, soft Italian polkas or zippy Scandinavian polkas. Polish polka bands are sprouting in Florida and California. Born in Bohemia in the 1830's, the polka spread quickly to Vienna, Paris and London. With its hopping, spinning movements, it was the rock and roll of its day until refined by classical composers. Immigrants brought it with them to America, but not until last year did the Grammy Awards include a polka category.

Jan 22. Pennsylvania State Treasurer R. Budd Dwyer, convicted on corruption charges, took his life today at a news conference.

N.Y. march protests black youth's death

Jan. 21. Chanting, waving placards, and wearing green ribbons, 3,000 paraders marched through Manhattan today, to protest against racial violence. The demonstrators were mourning Michael Griffith, a young black man hit and killed by a car a month ago in the Howard Beach section of Queens, as he fled from a gang of whites.

However, black shoppers apparently ignored calls by organizers for a city-wide boycott of white businesses. "I see no sense in it," said one black woman. "All they are doing is continuing the white beating up on black and the black beating up on white." But a white storekeeper was sympathetic. He said, "They're doing it because they are mad, and I agree with them" (→ 24).

Amy Carter charged in anti-CIA protest

Jan. 19. Amy Carter, the 19-year-old daughter of former President Jimmy Carter, and 14 others, including Abbie Hoffman, have been charged with trespassing and disorderly conduct for their part in a demonstration against the Central Intelligence Agency last November at the University of Massachusetts at Amherst, where Miss Carter is a sophomore. Amy Carter has been arrested three times before for protesting apartheid in South Africa. In this case, she and the others believe that "crimes by the CIA" justified their actions (→ 4/15).

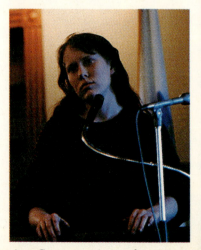
Amy Carter, growing up fast.

B-1 bomber: They call it the flying Edsel

The B-1, first tested in 1974, flew over twice the speed of sound.

Jan 19. More problems are reported with the B-1B bomber, the most expensive aircraft ever built. The Defense Department has requested $600 million to correct defects that range from leaky fuel tanks to major bugs in the B-1B's advanced electronic systems. The Air Force is withholding $300 million from contractors for shoddy work. Designed to penetrate Soviet air defenses, the B-1B is overweight with poor maneuverability and excessive fuel consumption. Critics call it a "flying Edsel," but the Air Force insists the B-1B can be made to work. It has ordered 100 of them at a cost of $283 million each.

Franchising trend is growing in America

Franchising is playing an increasingly large role in our economy, being the ticket to business ownership for many who lack much capital or experience. Last year, there were 478,452 franchise outlets in America, employing 6.3 million persons. Whereas fast food used to be the bulk of franchising, today's field covers an area from windshield wipers to cinnamon buns. Services are taking the lead. Venture magazine has picked sitters for pets, plants and people; aerobics; and medical and banking services as possible hot new areas.

$1 billion provided to retrain workers

Jan 19. In his budget for fiscal 1988, President Reagan would triple funds for the states to retrain jobless workers and help them find work. The $1 billion Worker Adjustment Assistance Program is seen as an alternative to Democratic moves to save jobs with protectionist legislation against foreign competition. The program favors training and re-employment over income support. Says a spokesman, "We want people to get back to work, not make it comfortable to be out of work." A hoped-for result: a more skilled labor force (→ 20).

Corporations using desktop publishing

Desktop publishing is revolutionizing office communications and saving money. With a personal computer, special software and a laser printer, companies can produce slick publications with elaborate graphics in-house. One recent desktop devotee says it took just six weeks to produce the same 250-page training manual that took three months last year. Independent publishers and graphic artists are the biggest users. At the end of 1985, there were 40,000 desktop systems in the U.S. and 1.6 million are expected to be in use in 1990.

Citizen sues to stop Idaho potato slogan

Jan 22. The "Famous Potatoes" slogan on Idaho automobile license plates has come under attack by one Boisean. Andrew Freese, a 23-year-old silver miner, claims it discriminates against other Idaho products, and he is suing the state to have it removed. Freese would prefer plates with no slogan, but if there had to be one, he would choose "Gem State," Idaho's official nickname. The Deputy Attorney General will move for a dismissal on the ground that the plaintiff has not been harmed by the existence of the slogan and therefore lacks standing to bring suit. A hearing is scheduled.

Schools blamed for competition failure

Jan 19. Longer school days and more of them (over 240 days in Japan compared to our 180 days a year), more emphasis on mathematics and sciences, hard work counting for more than innate ability, higher pay and more respect for teachers, greater involvement of the family, more homework and much less television watching — these are some of the explanations given for the sobering fact that primary and secondary schoolchildren, especially in Japan, West Germany and Russia, rank higher on international tests than American children.

Dating services are thriving in China

The Chinese call them introduction rooms, and the over-30 set flocks to them to fill out applications for desired spouses. Tall men (5'7" and over) are wanted by the women. If short, a college diploma helps. One's own housing is of crucial importance. In days past, people used to look for each other in the "love corner" of People's Parks. This practice has been banned as bordering on auctioneering with hawkers shouting "one, aged 34, looking for a 28-year-old." The new introduction rooms fill a definite social need in China.

Jan 19. George Shultz and Coretta King sing "We Shall Overcome" to mark Martin Luther King's birthday. But ten states failed to observe it (→ 20).

Jan 21. B.B. King, "King of the Blues," entered Rock and Roll's Hall of Fame today along with Smokey Robinson and Bill Haley.

JANUARY
Week 5 1987

Su	Mo	Tu	We	Th	Fr	Sa
				1	2	3
4	5	6	7	8	9	10
11	12	13	14	15	16	17
18	19	20	21	22	23	24
25	26	27	28	29	30	31

25. U.S.: Study shows poverty rising sharply among urban blacks (→ 2/10).

25. Melbourne: Stefan Edberg beats Pat Cash 6-3, 6-4, 3-6, 5-7, 6-3 for Australian Open title.

25. Bonn: Chancellor Kohl's center-right coalition holds power narrowly in vote (→ 6/14).

25. London: 180 injured in clash with police as 12,000 protest loss of 5,500 jobs in publishing.

26. Argentina: Nation paralyzed by 24-hour general strike against economic policies (→ 4/6).

27. Tokyo: Japan to renew auto export curbs in effort to head off protectionism in U.S. (→ 2/14).

28. Washington: Roger Boisjoly, engineer who opposed shuttle flight, sues Morton Thiokol, charging criminal homicide.

28. Tehran: Hojatolislam Rafsanjani, speaker of Iranian Parliament, justifies Beirut abductions as self-defense (→ 30).

28. Managua: American Sam Nesley Hall released, held since last month for spying (→ 2/9).

28. Washington: Shultz meets with Oliver Tambo, head of African National Congress (→ 2/7).

28. Madrid: Spain offers concessions in bid to defuse worst student unrest in decade (→ 6/11).

29. Washington: Senate panel charges admin. with deception in Iran-contra affair (→ 2/2).

29. U.S.: AT&T posts $1.7 billion loss for quarter (→ 30).

29. Boston: Dr. Jane Anderson wins $150,000 libel suit over Sylvia Plath's "The Bell Jar."

29. Philadelphia: Malcolm Arnold's "Big Overture for 3 Vacuum Cleaners, Floor Polisher, Organ and Full Orchestra" performed; conductor William Smith directs with a gun.

29. Mexico City: Thousands of students shut National Autonomous University, declaring it "first free territory in Mexico."

30. "Outrageous Fortune," with Bette Midler, and Woody Allen's "Radio Days" open today.

31. Newark, N.J.: People Express flies last flights before absorption into Continental Air.

Cory's troops put down Marcos uprising

Besieged from right and left, Philippine police arrest a demonstrator.

Jan 29. Government troops loyal to Philippine President Corazon Aquino fired tear gas into a Manila radio and television station this morning. A few minutes later, the mutineers who had occupied the facility for two days surrendered. Most of them support former President Ferdinand Marcos, and their rebellion has increased tensions in the Aquino government.

The rebels launched a wave of attacks on military and broadcasting installations on Tuesday. Today, General Fidel V. Ramos said the military is in control. Many of his officers, however, sympathize with the rebels and believe that Aquino is not dealing hard enough with Communist opponents (→ 2/2).

Evangelist receives money to save his life

Jan 26. You would never guess it, but all of his ills are economic. Three weeks ago, the Rev. Oral Roberts appeared before his massive television congregation and said, "I'm asking you to help extend my life," poignantly adding in the third person, "We're at the point where God could call Oral Roberts home in March." Since then, donations have poured in. In fact, while Roberts, 68, is in perfect health, his evangelical empire is not. Oral Roberts University, in Tulsa, Oklahoma, has been forced to shut down partially, and one ratings service finds Roberts' TV viewership has dropped 50% in ten years (→ 3/23).

Roberts and wife, Evelyn: Media does "devil's work" in criticizing fund-raiser.

Gorbachev asks for greater democracy

Jan 29. Soviet leader Mikhail S. Gorbachev called for greater democracy in the Communist Party, which he said had been largely responsible for economic and social stagnation in the Soviet Union. In a speech before a plenary meeting of the party's Central Committee, he urged greater "control from below" by giving voters a choice of candidates in elections for local government bodies. Coming on top of his campaign for market-style economic experiments and greater freedom of debate, his focus on party reform marked an important turning point in his program of "reconstruction" (→ 2/10).

Mikhail Gorbachev, Soviet leader.

Steel makers face heaviest losses yet

Jan 30. Record losses have been reported by America's two largest steel companies, the USX Corporation and the LTV Corporation. LTV today reported a loss of $435 million in the fourth quarter of 1986, while USX lost $1.41 billion.

LTV made money on its steel operations but had to set aside $600 million to pay creditors after it filed for protection under Chapter 11 of the Bankruptcy Code last year.

USX, formerly United States Steel, blamed its loss on the expenses of fighting off a takeover bid by Carl C. Icahn and on a six-month strike by the United Steelworkers. USX said it would sell $1.5 billion in assets over two years to return to profitability. Another record loss was reported by AT&T, which was $1.7 billion in the red last quarter (→ 2/2).

Rape is growing as issue on campuses

Jan 25. "Date rape" it is called, a sexual assault by someone the victim knows. Tomorrow, Wesleyan University in Middletown, Connecticut, will consider disciplining six students who dared to inform prospective freshmen about assaults on campus. The protesters thought incoming students should know about the dangers — as many as 30 women each semester may be raped, they claim. Mary Koss, a psychologist at Kent State University, believes the protesters and does not think Wesleyan is unique among American colleges. She says 90 percent of rape victims never notify authorities about attacks.

Television depicts businessmen as evil

The American businessman is television's most popular villain. Only outright criminals commit more crimes than a full third of the small screen's business executives. On an average of 14 times a week, one of them murders, steals, lies and cheats on prime-time TV. J.R. Ewing of "Dallas" and Alexis Carrington of "Dynasty" may lead the pack, but evil bankers have been offered lately on "Miami Vice," bribing and murdering businessmen on "Spenser for Hire," a toxic waste-dumping toy manufacturer on "Cagney and Lacey" and so on. What do real-life businessmen do about this image? Switch channels!

Ruined Angkor Wat is being resurrected

Ornate Angkor Wat was built in the 12th century for the spirit of a dead king.

Torture death arouses Korean opposition

Jan 30. When South Korean students clashed with police in Seoul this week, some carried firebombs. Others displayed pictures of Park Jong Chul, the new symbol of the resistance. Park, a student, died two weeks ago while in police custody. Authorities have since admitted that he was tortured in a tub of water. That admission has unified the students and put the government of President Chun Doo Hwan on the defensive. Several officials have been forced to resign (→ 2/7).

Jan 30. Surprisingly, the violent regime of Pol Pot wrought little damage on the archeological wonders of the ancient capital of Cambodia, Angkor Wat. While a few bullet holes pockmark the faces of sandstone gods and goddesses, the city's real enemies have been natural ones — time, water seepage, bat excrement and disfiguring algae.

Now, a team of Indian archeologists, at the invitation of the Khmer government, is starting to restore this vast monument to Hinduism. Founded in the 12th century, Angkor Wat houses an astounding number of pyramids, moats, libraries and galleries spreading over 40 square miles. Total reconstruction may take a decade.

African politics cause terrible infant deaths

Jan 31. Angola and Mozambique have the world's highest infant and child mortality rates, according to a report by UNICEF. The report, which examines the socioeconomic effects of fighting in the nine nations nearest South Africa, was originally an internal document, but UNICEF officials found it "so alarming" they made it public. In the two nations, the mortality rate for children under five is more than 325 for each 1,000 children. The rising death rates are due mostly to war-related economic destabilization and Pretoria's drive to keep the region economically dependent on South Africa.

Terry Waite missing

Jan 30. United States intelligence reports suggest that Terry Waite, a representative of the Anglican Church who had been negotiating for the release of two Americans held hostage in Lebanon, has been kidnapped by Shiite Moslems. The reports said it was unclear why Waite had been taken (→ 2/9).

Kids flunking gym

Jan 26. Nine out of ten American parents believe that their children are in good physical shape, but the head of the President's Council of Physical Fitness says that their condition is a "disgrace." George Allen took issue with a Louis Harris poll of parents by saying, "kids have no strength, no endurance."

In Mozambique a few faces still smile despite the toll of civil war and poverty.

Tom Berenger plays a scarred and cynical officer in Oliver Stone's new look at Vietnam, "Platoon."

Jan 25. Giants coach Bill Parcells gets a ritual bath after their 39-20 Super Bowl win over Denver.

Su	Mo	Tu	We	Th	Fr	Sa
1	2	3	4	5	6	7
8	9	10	11	12	13	14
15	16	17	18	19	20	21
22	23	24	25	26	27	28

2. Washington: N.Y. Times reports Pentagon aides knew of $1 bil. in private arms deals with Iran as early as 1983 (→ 2).

2. Washington: William J. Casey quits CIA; Deputy Director Robert M. Gates named to succeed (→ 3).

2. Houston: Training begins for new space shuttle crew (→ 19).

2. Manila: New constitution approved in referendum (→ 7).

3. Washington: Pat Buchanan resigns as White House communications director.

3. Washington: U.S. aides reveal Saudis agreed in 1981 to aid anti-Communist movements in return for AWAC planes (→ 10).

4. Pittsburgh: USX to shut three plants, cut 3,700 jobs.

4. Madonna gets fifth No. 1 hit with "Open Your Heart."

4. Armando Fernandez, ex-official in Chilean secret police, confesses to 1976 murder of Orlando Letelier (→ 3/18).

4. U.S. bars plan for nuclear-free zone in South Pacific (→ 5/14).

5. Mercury, Nevada: 438, including six congressmen, arrested in protest at nuclear test site.

5. Florida: Carlos Enrique Rivas extradited from Colombia as one of world's biggest drug dealers.

6. Zurich: U.S. reporter Gerald Seib arrives, expelled from Iran after being held six days (→ 12).

6. N.Y.: U.N. conference on population warns of rapid urban growth in Third World (→ 13).

6. N.Y.: Public Health Council outlaws smoking in most public indoor areas (→ 23).

7. Manila: On eve of end of 60-day cease-fire, rebels reject extension of truce (→ 10).

7. Washington: State Dept. tells Congress U.S. is dependent on South Africa for strategic minerals (→ 10).

7. Tampa Bay: Florida's new $230 mil., 4.1-mile Sunshine Skyway Bridge dedicated.

DEATH

4. Carl R. Rogers, founder of client-centered approach to psychotherapy (*1/8/1902).

Congress shows interest in homelessness

A makeshift dining room is one man's only shot at interior decorating.

Feb 6. As frigid winds whip through much of the nation, one sees shivering men and women huddled on steam grates or wrapped in rags as they seek warmth in city doorways. They are America's homeless, the street people whose numbers have been estimated to be anywhere from 250,000 to as high as three million. Some were once in mental hospitals, others once led normal lives but lost their jobs in a changing economy.

Now, help may be on its way, as Congress turns its attention to a problem so reminiscent of those days of the Great Depression of the 1930's. Already, Congress has sent to President Reagan a bill to provide $50 million in immediate aid to the homeless, and that may be only the beginning. Also pending are bills to provide $500 million to $4 billion in additional aid over the next two years.

The plight of the homeless was poignantly illustrated during the recent holidays by a statue placed in front of the Capitol by the Committee for Creative Nonviolence. It depicted homeless people sleeping on a steaming grate (→ 7/22).

Takeovers subside after 1986 frenzy

Feb 1. High stock prices, tax law changes and a lingering cloud from the Ivan Boesky scandal have helped to stop a corporate takeover spree, Wall Street observers say. There have been only 28 takeovers so far this year, compared to 93 in the last quarter of 1986. The stock market boom has made it harder to find corporate bargains, while the new tax law makes it more expensive to break up a company and sell its divisions after a takeover. Lessened activity by the Wall Street firm of Drexel Burnham Lambert, the biggest issuer of so-called junk bonds, in the wake of the Boesky scandal, has made it harder for takeover artists to find financing. A stock market drop will revive takeovers, experts say (→ 17).

Feb 4. Skipper Dennis Conner, in the South Pacific today, beat Australia's Kookaburra III 4-0 to bring the America's Cup back to the United States once again.

Longest steel strike in history concluded

Feb 2. Union workers began returning to USX Corporation mills today as the longest strike in steel industry history came to an end. The strike had kept 21,000 workers off the job since last August 1. It was ended by union acceptance of a four-year contract that will give workers an average of $1 an hour less in pay but that could restore at least 2,000 jobs that have been farmed out to contractors. The new contract will save the company $300 million or more over the next four years. As part of the agreement, nearly 2,700 older workers will retire and 1,346 younger union members will be recalled from layoffs (→ 4).

Flashy but talented Liberace succumbs

Feb 4. Liberace, the most flamboyant of popular pianists, died today at age 67 in his block-long palace in Palms Springs, California, officially of a brain disease, unofficially of AIDS.

Spectators were drawn to the extravagant showman as much by how he looked as how he sounded. His sequined wardrobe included a $300,000 blue-fox cape with a 16-foot train worthy of one who annually earned $5 million for 25 years. Flanked by candelabras, he played what he called "Reader's Digest versions" of familiar music, and his 37-second version of Chopin's "Minute Waltz" was but one example of his avowed secret of "cutting out the dull parts."

Liberace, the king of kitsch.

Thousands in Seoul protest torture death

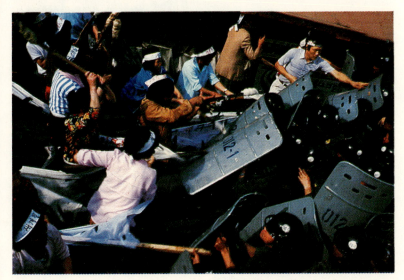

Angry protesters put Seoul riot police on the defensive with hit-and-run tactics.

Feb 7. A large police force, estimated at 35,000 officers, attacked a mostly peaceful student demonstration in Seoul today. South Korean authorities also charged crowds in three other cities. Nearly 600 people were arrested. The demonstrations were organized to protest the torture death in mid-January of a student in police custody.

In Seoul, some students threw gasoline bombs at riot police. But eyewitnesses say most of the violence was initiated by authorities. One group of students, their eyes closed in prayer, was pelted with tear gas grenades. Others sang hymns as they were arrested.

The national police chief tried to justify his officers' actions by saying, "Today's illegal assemblies, if left unchecked, could have caused radical disturbances and riots."

Opposition leader Kim Dae Jung, who was prevented from attending one of the rallies, said, "We are indignant at the barbarous activities of the government directed at a people in mourning." Another opposition spokesman warned that "police overreaction" only creates new unrest (→ 3/7).

New CBS boss seeks to cut news $50m

Feb 5. Laurence Tisch, Chief Executive at CBS, is aiming his budget-cutting ax directly at the news division. Tisch refuses to talk specifics, but he has reportedly asked CBS News President Howard Stringer to slice his budget by $50 million, or 17 percent. The directive may cost hundreds of employees their jobs. It also ends the special status the news division has developed within the network.

Many news producers and correspondents were heard grumbling today about Tisch's insensitivity. But Stringer defended the "slimming down to a smaller, more efficient operation." The CBS News budget has more than tripled in the past nine years, to nearly $300 million a year (→ 3/16).

Haiti still in agony year after uprising

Feb 6. A year after the ouster of dictator Jean-Claude "Baby Doc" Duvalier, Haiti remains the poorest country in the Western hemisphere with little hope in sight for the immediate future.

Violent crime is up, unemployment over 50 percent, and hunger the rule. The land is awash in smuggled goods, and tourism has vanished. Though police brutality is no longer official, ill-trained forces have killed a number of civilians with panicky gunfire. Still, no one would turn back the clock as Haitians freely voice their opinions and criticize the provisional government, which is gamely trying to plan democratic elections in November with a largely illiterate electorate (→ 3/30).

Met opens new wing for 20th Century art

Feb 3. The Lila Acheson Wallace Wing in the Metropolitan Museum of Art was opened today, confirming New York's reputation as a great modern art showcase. Unlike the Guggenheim Museum, the wing does not vie with its art but accommodates it. Lila Acheson Wallace, who donated the wing, was the wife of DeWitt Wallace and co-founder with him of the Reader's Digest.

Marsden Hartley's "Portrait of a German Officer" (1914) is one of many early 20th Century works in the wing's healthy collection. While there are as yet only a few examples of Futurism or Expressionism, the sparseness of the collection in the wing's 50,000 square feet indicates there will be additions.

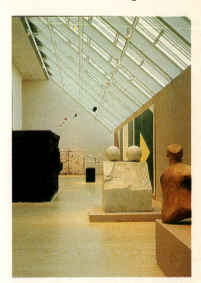

Sculpture gallery in the new wing.

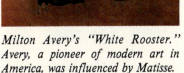

Milton Avery's "White Rooster." Avery, a pioneer of modern art in America, was influenced by Matisse.

"Portrait of a German Officer."

French painter Pierre Bonnard's "The Terrace at Vernon." Oil on canvas.

Su	Mo	Tu	We	Th	Fr	Sa
1	2	3	4	5	6	7
8	9	10	11	12	13	14
15	16	17	18	19	20	21
22	23	24	25	26	27	28

8. Washington: Shultz rules out decision on S.D.I. deployment for two years (→ 21).

8. U.S.: Medical costs up 7.7% in 1986, rising 7 times faster than Consumer Price Index (→ 12).

9. New York: Paul Klee exhibit opens at Museum of Modern Art.

9. Washington: Americas Watch charges contras with continued human rights abuses (→ 16).

9. Beirut: 17 killed by car bomb; kidnappers of U.S. educators extend deadline for release of 400 Israeli-held Arab prisoners (→ 17).

9. Washington: Reagan endorses plan to bar federal aid to groups that counsel on abortion.

10. New York: Three whites charged with murder in Howard Beach racial attack (→ 14).

10. Moscow: Soviets pardon 140 political prisoners (→ 12).

10. Washington: Reagan admin. panel finds constructive engagement in South Africa a failure, suggests intl. sanctions (→ 12).

10. The Philippines: 17 civilians killed by govt. troops during search for leftist rebels (→ 3/2).

12. New York: Robert Freeman, Richard Wigton, Timothy Tabor, leading Wall St. brokers, held for insider trading (→ 20).

12. Washington: Reagan proposes expansion of Medicare to cover catastrophic illness.

12. Washington: Survey shows winning senators spent avg. of $3 million on 1986 campaigns.

12. Cape Town: Govt. acknowledges it has jailed black children under 11 years of age (→ 20).

12. Geneva: U.N. report claims Iran has executed 7,000 since shah left in 1979 (→ 5/5).

13. Nairobi: "Safe Motherhood" conference ends, reporting 99% of deaths during childhood occur in Third World.

14. Washington: Klanwatch Project reports 45 cases of arson and cross-burnings in last two years after blacks moved into white neighborhoods (→ 25).

14. Harare, Zimbabwe: Paul Simon and South African musicians play to crowd of 20,000.

Police in Moscow end rallies by dissidents

The streets of Moscow, opening up to the expression of discontent.

Feb 12. Three days of demonstrations by Jewish refuseniks and other dissidents in Moscow have been ended by Soviet officials, calling into question the scope and effectiveness of Soviet leader Mikhail Gorbachev's campaign for reform.

Three days ago, the first demonstration in the capital without interference from Soviet authorities was held, but yesterday the dissidents were dispersed as usual by police.

Last week, Gorbachev delivered a speech to the Central Committee in which he expanded upon his goal of a transformation of Soviet society which would speed up the nation's sluggish economic growth and modernize its institutions. He said that "democratization" means drawing "into the reorganization its decisive force — the people."

Meanwhile, Gorbachev's ideas have had a mixed response in Eastern Europe. In East Germany and Czechoslovakia, there is resistance to change. Hungary remains circumspect, while in Poland, the leaders have echoed most closely the new concepts of reform (→ 16).

French designers show shorter dresses

The spring fashions of Paris, by French designer Maryll Lanvin.

Feb 9. In the eyes of fashion designers, today's woman is ready to turn the clock back 20 years and hike up her hemline again. What else could account for the designer shows in Paris this week featuring above-the-knee dresses in the forms of poufs and parabolas? These strictly impractical dresses are favored by Christian Dior, Yves Saint Laurent and many smaller fashion houses.

Ruffles and bows are in, as well as lavish petticoats adding fullness to skirts. Some crinolines are made to billow in back; bustles may be right around the corner. Colors for these frocks are not too surprising, considering they are offered for spring: wide-eyed pinks, greens and pastels. And the fabrics are satin, taffeta and others suited to feminine whimsy (→ 5/18).

Koop urges fighting AIDS with condoms

Feb 10. Saying that the growing threat of AIDS makes protective action necessary, Surgeon General C. Everett Koop today called for condom advertisements on television. Appearing before a House subcommittee, Dr. Koop said condoms offered the best protection against the AIDS virus for those "who will not practice abstinence or monogamy." Several Republican members of the subcommittee said Dr. Koop's advice would encourage an overly permissive lifestyle. Representatives of all three major television networks said condom advertisements would offend many viewers. Koop said condom advertising would have a "public health benefit" (→ 3/3).

The condom: no longer taboo?

Texaco fined $8.5b for Getty oil action

Feb 12. A Texas state appeals court today upheld all but $2 billion of a $10.53 billion jury award against Texaco Inc. for thwarting a takeover of the Getty Oil Company by the Pennzoil Company and taking over Getty itself. The ruling confirmed an award of $7.35 billion in compensatory damages voted by a district court jury but reduced punitive damages by $2 billion. The damages "are supported by the evidence and were not the result of mere passion, prejudice or improper motive," the appeals court said. Texaco said it would appeal the award "if necessary, to the United States Supreme Court." The company insists it did not know of a contract between Pennzoil and Getty, but the jury rejected this (→ 4/12).

One million killed in Iran-Iraq fighting

Feb 9. Casualties in the Iran-Iraq war now total about one million, according to Western military sources who have followed the course of the war since it began in September 1980. They estimate that of this total perhaps 650,000 are Iranian.

The Iranians have been on the offensive since early 1982. Tens of thousands of half-trained schoolboys have been thrown into mass attacks against fortified Iraqi positions and suffered heavy losses.

Meanwhile, the Iranian air force, made up largely of American planes bought by the deposed Shah, has been whittled away by Iraqi attacks and poor maintenance.

But Iran, with roughly three times as many people as its enemy, continues to base its strategy on a "final offensive" that will defeat Iraq and topple the government of Saddam Hussein.

Iraq's strategy is to defend its second city of Basra and to employ a superior air force against Iran's oil industry and petroleum exports which support the war effort. This has been partially successful (→ 3/23).

Islamic militants in Iran sell their revolution on the face of postage stamps.

Boston exhibit highlights use of robots

The robot: Will it bring luxury or unemployment to humans in the future?

Feb 9. Robots that paint pictures, play cards, pour chemicals and scoot through rooms are on display this week at the Boston Museum of Science in a $4 million exhibition, "Robots and Beyond." More than three dozen intelligent machines are in the exhibition, which will travel to seven other cities in the next three years.

Visitors are greeted by a robot named Jorel, who announces, "Humans, you are witnessing the beginning of a great new era." They can move on to test a patch of artificial "skin" outfitted with a film that transforms a touch into an electrical signal; hit it rapidly, and the robot exclaims, "Hey! Cut it out! What are you, a woodpecker?"

The exhibition also includes a tic-tac-toe program that uses the stored judgments of seven specialized computer programs. While the exhibition is mostly for fun, it is an introduction to the growing commercial world of robots. About 50 companies are marketing "automated guided vehicles," mobile robots for the factory or office.

Iran affair leads to suicide attempt

Feb 10. Robert C. McFarlane, the former national security adviser who played a central role in the decision to sell arms to Iran, apparently tried to commit suicide by taking an overdose of tranquilizers. The former Marine Lieutenant Colonel was rushed by ambulance from his home in suburban Maryland to the Bethesda Naval Hospital, where he was reported to be recovering. According to his wife and lawyer, McFarlane, after writing what was described as a garbled note, took 30 to 40 Valium tablets during the night. McFarlane, who had testified before congressional panels on his role in arranging for the arms sales to Iran, was described by friends as depressed over having failed the President (→ 19).

Japanese influx is changing Midwest

Feb 14. Weed-filled lots are turned into auto plants and sushi is replacing pizza in small-town America as a record number of Japanese are moving into the industrial Middle West. A Mazda plant between Detroit and Toledo; a Chrysler-Mitsubishi plant in Bloomington, Illinois; a Honda plant in Marysville, Ohio; a Fuji-Isuzu plant in Lafayette, Indiana, are being completed. The Japan Detroit Press prints a monthly newspaper. Daily non-stop flights between Detroit and Tokyo begin in May. Some see a paradox in all of this, remembering that a few years ago the region was frozen by recession and plant closings, often blamed on the aggressiveness of the Japanese auto industry (→ 17).

Japan steel maker cuts back sharply

Feb 13. Echoing the problems that hit the American steel industry several years ago, the Nippon Steel Corporation today said it would shut down five blast furnaces and cut 19,000 jobs over the next four years. Nippon, the world's leading steelmaker, said it would not dismiss any workers. Instead, it said 9,000 employees would retire, 6,000 would be shifted to other divisions and other, unspecified arrangements would be made for the last 4,000. Nippon said it had to make the cuts because it would lose $650 million in this fiscal year. Just as American steel plants have lost business to more efficient Japanese mills, Japanese steelmakers are being underpriced by Korea, where wage costs are low.

Feb 11. Cold War on ice: The U.S. All-Stars edge a traveling Soviet team 4-3 in Quebec.

Su	Mo	Tu	We	Th	Fr	Sa
1	2	3	4	5	6	7
8	9	10	11	12	13	14
15	16	17	18	19	20	21
22	23	24	25	26	27	28

15. Daytona Beach, Fla: Bill Elliott wins Daytona 500.

16. L.A.: Reagan admin. charged with reviving McCarthy-era law to deport eight Palestinians for alleged tie to radical group.

16. Miami: Adolfo Calero resigns as leader of contras in effort to unify rebels (→ 3/9).

17. New York: Dow Jones climbs 54.14 to 2,237.49, despite insider trading scandals (→ 27).

17. Washington: James Webb, who called Vietnam Memorial a "wailing wall for future anti-draft and anti-nuclear demonstrators," named to replace John Lehman as secretary of Navy.

17. Beirut: 24 die in clash between Shiites and alliance of Druse and Communists (→ 18).

17. Albuquerque: Michelle Renee Royer, Miss Texas, wins Miss U.S.A. beauty pageant.

18. New York: Amnesty International announces drive against death penalty in U.S. (→ 4/22).

19. Washington: McFarlane, in hospital bed, tells of memo to provide Reagan "plausible deniability" on Iran deal (→ 20).

19. Boston: Researchers report defective gene is one cause of Alzheimer's disease.

19. Washington: Carl Sagan tells Senate a trip to Mars would revitalize space program (→ 5/27).

19. Florida: Vida Blue, pitcher, retires from baseball.

19. Washington: Reagan lifts economic sanctions on Poland, citing release of political prisoners (→ 4/1).

19. Dublin: Charles Haughey's Fianna Fail party wins vote, but is three seats short of a majority.

20. White Plains, N.Y.: Dennis Levine gets two years, $362,000 fine for insider trading (→ 4/6).

20. N.Y.: U.S., U.K. veto U.N. call for mandatory sanctions on South Africa (→ 4/2).

21. Washington: Scientists link antibiotics in animal feed to salmonella poisoning in humans.

21. Washington: Officials say Reagan has barred discussion of S.D.I. at Geneva (→ 26).

New superconductive compound is found

Feb 15. American scientists today announced discovery of a material that loses all electrical resistance at higher temperatures than ever before achieved — an advance with immense implications for science and technology. Physicists Paul C. W. Chu of the University of Houston and Mau-Kuen Wu of the University of Alabama said the new material becomes superconducting at 283 degrees below zero Fahrenheit, or 98 degrees above zero on the Celsius scale.

The discovery was based on the work of J. Georg Bednorz and K. Alex Mueller of the IBM Zurich Research Laboratories in Switzerland. It means that physicists can do superconductivity research using cheap liquid nitrogen, instead of the lower temperatures that require expensive liquid helium. Potential applications range from ultrafast

Superconductor floats atop magnet.

computers to magnetically levitated trains. Chu said he will not disclose the composition of the new material until a patent is filed (→ 3/20).

Japan analyzes U.S. failure to compete

Feb 17. A loss of management effectiveness in basic industries is one major reason for the American loss of competitiveness in world markets, a new Japanese study says. Other reasons are poor labor relations and failure to adapt to changes in industrial technology, says the report of the Japanese Foreign Trade Council, composed of exporters.

The United States still has many strengths, including a dynamic market, reduced wage costs and technological superiority in many advanced fields, the Japanese say. But failure to develop laboratory advances into commercial products puts the United States in danger of becoming a "hamburger stand economy" based on service industries and raw materials, the report says.

The study adds that aging factories in the Midwest and Northeast cannot supply the needs of fast-growing states in the Sun Belt, leading to a growing reliance on imports. But more than half of America's 1,000 largest firms now have major cost-cutting programs to improve competitiveness (→ 3/9).

Japan leads in exports while the U.S. is plagued by a soaring trade deficit.

50 more killed in Beirut; 120 injured

Feb 18. As otherwise peaceful, civilian neighborhoods smoulder from tank and heavy artillery fire, two days of brutal fighting in Moslem West Beirut have claimed 50 dead and 120 wounded.

Though daily battles have become commonplace during the 12-year civil war, the past 48 hours have seen an unparalleled rise in firepower as hundreds of armed militiamen roam the streets. Described as "a fight to the finish to control West Beirut," it pits the Shiite Amal movement and the Lebanese army's mostly Shiite Sixth Brigade against the Druse Progressive Socialist Party and the Lebanese Communist Party. Hussein Mrowe, a ranking member of the latter, was gunned down in front of his family (→ 22).

A fighter catches the Rambo spirit.

ABC's "Amerika" causes controversy

Feb 18. In 1983, ABC made the mistake of showing a film called "The Day After," dealing with the effects of a nuclear war. Some conservatives demanded equal time, and "Amerika" is paying for it now. The 14 and one-half-hour mini-series, airing this week, follows the trials and tribulations of a Nebraska farm family after a Russian invasion. "Amerika," which stars Kris Kristofferson, has angered peace activists and, of course, the Soviet Union. ABC is upset too — after the first night, the ratings plummeted.

Alfonsin brings Argentine rebellion to end

The Argentine military, now under fire for the "dirty war" of the 1970's.

April 20. The Argentine military crisis ended without bloodshed today when rebel officers surrendered to President Raul Alfonsin. Alfonsin flew to the army base where the rebellion began and talked to the mutineers, who said they recognized the president as commander-in-chief and did not want to overthrow the government.

The drama began four days ago when an army major would not go to court to face charges of human rights abuses. He is one of 280 military men who have charges pending against them in civilian courts for their actions during the so-called dirty war, Argentina's crackdown against leftists in the 1970's. Many lower-level officers believe they should not be held responsible because they were following orders. The officers who took part in the mutiny will be prosecuted.

O'Toole makes bow on New York stage

April 25. America will not be welcoming Peter O'Toole back to Broadway tonight—he's never been there before. His appearance in "Pygmalion" is his Broadway debut. However, the actor, 54, is no stranger to the London stage, having played Henry Higgins there.

O'Toole, hypnotic onstage and off.

Central American policy is protested

April 25. As many as 100,000 people filled the streets of Washington, D.C., today, stretched out along a route between the White House and the Capitol, in a giant 1960's-style demonstration staged to protest United States involvement in Central America.

Although Lane Kirkland, President of the AFL-CIO, had tried to persuade unions to stay away from the rally, nearly a third of the marchers displayed union placards or insignia. Many other marchers represented church groups or were volunteers who have spent time in Nicaragua, helping with the coffee harvest or building schools. Today's protest was a prelude to civil disobedience planned for April 27. Five to six hundred demonstrators intend to get arrested at that time, including Daniel Ellsberg, Amy Carter and Abbie Hoffman (→ 27).

Experts say "Star Wars" is distant dream

War in space: Still just the fantasy of Hollywood producers and moviegoers?

April 22. A panel of leading physicists appointed to study the advanced weapon systems needed for the "Star Wars" anti-missile program has concluded that at least a decade of intense research is needed to determine whether any of them will work effectively. The report of a 42-member committee of the American Physical Society is a severe blow to proponents of the Strategic Defense Initiative, as the Reagan administration calls it.

Supporters of the missile defense system have maintained that it could build a shield over the United States in the foreseeable future. But the new report said there are "significant gaps" in scientific and technical knowledge about the needed technologies, adding that it is "highly questionable" whether a Star Wars system could survive an enemy attack. The conclusion was reached after the panel received classified briefings about laser and particle beam weapons being developed as essential components of a missile defense system.

The Defense Department called these conclusions "subjective and unduly pessimistic about our capability to bring to fruition the specific technologies" for S.D.I. (→ 6/1).

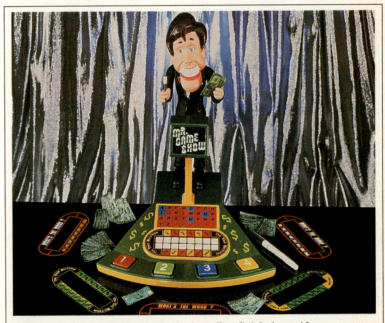

For all the kids in TV land who look to Pat Sajak for guidance, one toy manufacturer has the latest in educational games: Mr. Gameshow.

Su	Mo	Tu	We	Th	Fr	Sa
			1	2	3	4
5	6	7	8	9	10	11
12	13	14	15	16	17	18
19	20	21	22	23	24	25
26	27	28	29	30		

27. U.S. Dept. of Interior announces plans to open millions of offshore acres to oil drilling.

27. Washington: Hundreds arrested at CIA offices in sit-down protest of U.S. foreign policy (→ 29).

27. Washington: U.S. bars Austrian Pres. Kurt Waldheim from entering U.S. due to Nazi activities in WWII (→ 28).

27. Sri Lanka: 400 reported dead in raids on Tamil bases (→ 6/5).

27. Zeebrugge, Belgium: Inquiry charges man responsible for closing doors was asleep when ferry sunk, killing at least 182.

28. Washington: Sen. Paul Laxalt declares candidacy for Republican nomination (→ 5/3).

28. Managua: Sandinistas announce Benjamin Linder, U.S. engineer working in Nicaragua, was killed by contras (→ 5/13).

28. Rome: Italian govt. falls; Parliament dissolved; elections called for June 14 (→ 7/2).

28. Washington: Supreme Court upholds "propaganda" label for three Canadian films on acid rain and nuclear war.

28. Algiers: PLO, ousted by Egypt, to move to Algeria, Iraq.

29. Washington: Carl R. Channell pleads guilty to defrauding govt. by raising tax-exempt funds to aid contras, citing North as co-conspirator (→ 5/1).

29. Moscow: Play featuring Bukharin and Trotsky is approved for publication (→ 30).

30. Washington: House, 290-137, passes trade bill requiring retaliation for foreign nations that close markets (→ 30).

30. Fort Meade, Md.: Army opens 24-hour hotline (1-800-CALL-SPY) to uncover spies.

30. Washington: Japanese P.M. Nakasone, on U.S. visit, tells Reagan Bank of Japan will help lower interest rates (→ 6/8).

30. N.Y.: Mayor Koch and deputy mayor of Peking introduce pandas Yong Yong and Ling Ling to public at Bronx Zoo.

30. L.A.: Playboy picks Southern Baptist Donna Edmonson, a self-professed virgin, as playmate of the year.

Soviet policy encouraging small business

Small businesses may improve the standard of living in the Soviet Union.

April 30. You might call it creeping capitalism. A new law goes into effect tomorrow in the Soviet Union which allows individuals to open their own businesses. There are many restrictions, and not everyone is sure how the new system will work. But it is clear that Mikhail Gorbachev is willing to take a few chances to improve goods and services and even introduce a little competition.

In cities like Riga, small entrepreneurs are taking advantage of the Gorbachev policy. New cafes and hairdressing salons are bustling. One man is seeking a permit to open pay toilets. Another is trying to heat up the cold Russian winters by becoming a matchmaker.

Soviets who want to open their own businesses cannot quit their state jobs. For the most part, they have to moonlight. In addition to working hard, they have to overcome social attitudes which have developed under Communism. As one woman put it, "Russians would rather be equally poor than see somebody else get rich" (→ 5/25).

Islamic revival is gaining ground in Israel

April 29. As Moslem demands for an "Islamic Palestine" counter Israeli claims to a "Greater Israel," a Moslem fundamentalist revival is taking root in Israel itself.

The movement traces its ironical

An Israeli Moslem near Jerusalem.

origins to the 1967 Israeli victory in the Six Day War, which opened for Israeli Arabs the Moslem holy places in Jerusalem and other Islamic centers of learning, making possible a renewed cultural connection with the Moslem past.

Taking a leaf from the success of Ayatollah Khomeini's 1978 Islamic Revolution, the movement turned briefly violent, within Israel, to achieve its political ends. Now advocating non-violence and hoping to achieve a grass-roots victory through the ballot box, it has turned its back on PLO leader Yasser Arafat and discredited the divisive results, within the Arab world, of Khomeini's tactics.

An Arab professor says Arab youths have turned to Islam because "Islam can't be broken. The Israelis can't take Islam away from me. I am right. They are wrong" (→ 5/12).

Waldheim is barred from entering U.S.

April 28. "I have a clear conscience," said Kurt Waldheim, responding to a United States Justice Department decision to place the Austrian President on its "watch list." The watch list is a compilation of the names of 40,000 people barred from entering the United States for reasons ranging from infectious disease to, in Waldheim's case, participating in persecution based on race, religion or political opinion. The former Secretary General of the United Nations is said to have belonged to a Nazi unit sending Jews to death camps in World War II (→ 6/25).

New York applauds Guinness' talents

April 27. Tonight at Avery Fisher Hall many personalities were honored, but only one man took a bow. Alec Guinness, masterful character actor, was the subject of the Lincoln Center Film Society's annual tribute to film achievement. Sir Alec's 55-year career has no lack of leading roles (he won an Oscar for his British colonel in "Bridge on the River Kwai" in 1957), but he is happiest behind a putty nose and a sham mustache.

Not every suburb is rich and elegant

April 29. If the word "suburb" conjures up images of comfortable living, take a look at East Chicago Heights, 25 miles south of Chicago, and recently renamed Ford Heights. It is America's poorest suburb with shuttered stores and crumbling houses, inhabited by 5,300 people with a per capita income of $4,523 and an umemployment rate of 55 percent. Among the country's ten poorest suburbs, five are predominantly black, including Ford Heights, and are near Chicago, Miami and St. Louis. The other five are towns with mainly Hispanic residents outside Los Angeles. The per capita income disparity between the richest and poorest suburbs was 9 to 1 in 1979.

MAY

Week 18-19 1987

Su	Mo	Tu	We	Th	Fr	Sa
3	4	5	6	7	1 8	2 9
10	11	12	13	14	15	16
17	18	19	20	21	22	23
24	25	26	27	28	29	30
31						

1. Washington: Iran-contra panels find U.S. got arms for contras from Poland and China (→ 3).

1. Miami: Honduran ex-army man says military kidnapped and killed up to 200 leftists between 1980 and 1984.

2. Louisville: Alysheba, at 8-1, wins Kentucky Derby with Chris McCarron riding (→ 16).

2. El Salvador: Leftists raid army base, killing 18 (→ 14).

3. Miami Herald publishes report alleging Gary Hart spent night with Donna Rice (→ 8).

3. N.Y.: Reagan, at Ellis Island, renews plea for contra aid (→ 5).

3. Munich: Pope acknowledges value of Protestant Reformation for renewal of Catholicism.

4. Washington: Supreme Court rules Rotary clubs must admit women (→ 7/2).

4. London: De Kooning's "Pink Lady" sold for $3.63 mil., tying record for living artist.

4. Towson, Md.: Ricky L. Gates, Conrail engineer, held for manslaughter in Amtrak crash.

5. Washington: Richard Secord, at start of hearings, says top officials helped in contra aid (→ 6).

5. Washington: Joint tribunal orders U.S. to return $451.4 mil. in frozen assets to Iran (→ 9/28).

5. U.S.: Thousands of aliens line up to apply for new status as amnesty program begins.

5. Mercury, Nevada: 98 arrested in protest at nuclear test site.

6. Washington: Justice Thurgood Marshall criticizes bicentennial fest, noting Constitution perpetuated slavery (→ 6/7).

6. Springfield, Missouri: Jim Bakker ousted from Pentecostal Assemblies of God (→ 15).

6. N.Y.: Two convicted of slashing face of model Marla Hanson (→ 9/28).

7. Washington: Stewart B. McKinney is first in Congress to die of AIDS (→ 15).

7. Oklahoma: Two indicted on charges of plotting to murder Nicaraguan Pres. Ortega (→ 11).

9. Warsaw: Polish jetliner crashes taking off for N.Y.; 183 killed.

Gary Hart out of race

May 8. Gary Hart's womanizing and his "monkey business" caught up with him today. The Colorado Democrat dropped out of the race for the presidential nomination. Hart made the announcement at a terse, occasionally defiant news conference in Denver less than a week after the Miami Herald linked him to Donna Rice, a 29-year-old model and part-time actress.

Hart did not mention Miss Rice, but he did charge that the press has become too concerned with the personal lives of candidates. "Too much of it is just a mockery," Hart said, "and if it continues to destroy people's integrity and honor, then that system will eventually destroy itself." The former Senator also said he was "angry and defiant."

Hart's supporters and critics will debate whether the media or Hart himself destroyed his candidacy. Rumors have circulated for years that Hart is a womanizer, and they were not dispelled by the revelation that he had taken a trip with Miss Rice on a yacht named "Monkey Business." Even Hart's supporters admit he invited more scrutiny of his personal life by telling The New York Times Magazine that reporters should follow him around.

The Miami Herald staked out a Washington house where Hart and Miss Rice allegedly spent the night. Hart's departure leaves five Democrats in the race, as well as Jesse Jackson, an undeclared candidate, who ranks highest in polls (→ 16).

Hart: Villain or media victim?

Donna Rice: In the eye of the storm.

Sailor goes around world in 134 days

May 7. After 27,000 miles aboard a single-hull sailboat, Philippe Jeantot of France arrived in Newport, R.I., as winner of the BOC Challenge race around the world, sponsored by the London-based gas firm, BOC. He arrived 134 days, five hours, 23 minutes, 56 seconds after a fleet of 25 boats set sail on August 30. His was the fastest time ever achieved by a single-hull craft. The French sailor will receive $15,000 in cash and a trophy. He lopped 24 days off his time in a 1983 race with the help of a boat that was four feet longer.

Butterfield of blues fame is dead at 44

May 4. Paul Butterfield, a musician whose wailing harmonica brought Chicago-style blues to a large white audience in the mid-60's, died today at 44 of an apparent drug overdose. Butterfield studied classical flute before falling under the spell in his teens of such legendary Chicago bluesmen as Muddy Waters and Howlin' Wolf. He founded the Paul Butterfield Blues Band soon afterwards with guitarist Mike Bloomfield. The group evolved a highly influential sound that combined elements of blues, rock, soul and Indian music.

Quebec agrees to Canada's basic law

May 1. Quebec has agreed to sign the Canadian Constitution after being assured it will be granted status as a "distinct society" within that nation. In his announcement today of the agreement, sought for 20 years, Canadian Prime Minister Brian Mulroney observed, "What we have now is a whole country." Announcement of the new accord was greeted by a standing ovation from all of the political parties in the House of Commons and with celebrations in many parts of Canada. However, the new agreement must be formally ratified by Canada's Parliament and by the provincial legislatures before it becomes final.

Ferry capsizes in China; 90 killed

May 8. Up to 90 people were killed today when a wooden ferry capsized after a collision with a tugboat on the Yangtze River in China. The ferry was bound from Nantong to Changshu with 96 passengers and four crew members when the collision occurred at 11:16 a.m. The vessel was two miles from shore, and only seven passengers have been rescued. The tugboat was not damaged by the collision.

May 3. Julius Erving ended a 16-year career today with 24.2 points per game and 10,525 rebounds.

Whites-only vote protested in South Africa

Anti-apartheid demonstrators fill the steps of Witwatersrand University.

May 6. Students at the University of Witwatersrand, a predominantly white school, defied South African police today by holding a demonstration to protest the impending whites-only election. Riot police arrested 120 students and fired tear gas at about 50 faculty members in Johannesburg.

The demonstration broke out after police banned a speech by Winnie Mandela, wife of the jailed African National Congress leader Nelson Mandela. To enforce the ban, hundreds of armed policemen charged into the midst of a crowd of 3,000 students who had gathered at the main university hall for the speech. Rather than disperse, the students began a chanting demonstration, regrouping each time after being charged by police using whips and rubber batons.

Faculty members watching the demonstration said they would support the students' demand for a two-day closing of the university to protest the white election. Police said they used tear gas after students began hurling stones (→ 6/3).

Ex-CIA chief dies as Iran inquiry goes on

Casey, CIA Director since 1981, may carry important secrets to his grave.

May 6. William J. Casey, who was Director of Central Intelligence during the Iran-contra affair, is dead of a brain tumor at age 74. His death came within hours after the first witness in congressional hearings had testifed that Casey assisted in providing arms to the Nicaraguan rebels at a time when Congress had banned military aid.

Casey was hospitalized on December 15, the day before he was to testify before a Senate committee on the CIA's role in the sale of American arms to Iran. He subsequently resigned from the CIA post that he had held from the start of the Reagan administration.

On Capitol Hill, there has been persistent speculation that Casey was a central figure in arranging for the arms sales to Iran and diversion of funds to the contras in Nicaragua, but his death may mean that his role will remain a mystery. A successful lawyer and investor, Casey is widely credited with having rebuilt the covert operations and intelligence-gathering capabilities of the CIA (→ 6).

200,000 rally in support of Soviet Jews

March 5. "Only when the last Jew is with us in freedom can we relax our struggle." Those were the words of Soviet dissident Natan Sharansky, at a rainy, outdoor rally attended by 200,000 in New York, on behalf of Jews barred from leaving the Soviet Union. Some demonstrators said they were relatives or friends of Soviet Jews who had been beaten or jailed because they wished to leave.

Sharansky now lives in Israel; until last year, his wife spoke for him at similar rallies, as he sought to leave the U.S.S.R. His presence today could be seen as a sign of an easing of Soviet emigration policy. But in his speech, he warned against false optimism in the struggle for Jewish emigration.

Some 1,400 Jews have been allowed to leave the U.S.S.R. since January, compared to 914 in 1986. But Jewish leaders are striving for the release of at least 51,000 a year, matching the high point of Soviet Jewish emigration, back in 1979.

Number of Soviet Jews allowed to emigrate

51,320

4,699

50,000

40,000

30,000

20,000

10,000

0

1978 '79 '80 '81 '82 '83 '84 '85 '86 '87

Note: 1987 figure is through August. Basic data: National Conference on Soviet Jewry.

Jewish-born nun is beatified by Pope

May 1. In Cologne, West Germany, Pope John Paul II today beatified Edith Stein, a Jewish-born Carmelite nun killed by the Nazis at Auschwitz. In the Roman Catholic Church, beatification is the last step before sainthood.

Some Jews, including members of Edith Stein's family, had criticized the move, saying she was martyred for her Jewish origins, not her adopted Christian faith.

The pope said, "Today, the church is honoring a daughter of Israel who remained faithful, as a Jew, to the Jewish people, and as a Catholic, to our crucified Lord Jesus Christ." But not all critics were allayed. A niece of Edith Stein noted that in 1933 her aunt had tried but failed to win the support of Pope Pius XI in defending Jews.

Reagan is named in diversion to contras

May 6. A retired Air Force general testified today that he had been told President Reagan knew that money from the arms sales to Iran was diverted to support the rebels in Nicaragua. Maj. Gen. Richard V. Secord told congressional committees that Lieut. Col. Oliver L. North, a former National Security Council aide, reported that in conversations with the president he had remarked that "it was very ironic that some of the Ayatollah's money was being used to support the contras." Secord, who was the main organizer of the Iran arms sales and support for the contras, said he did not know whether North was joking, but added, "I did not take it as a joke." Reagan has maintained he was unaware of diversion of funds to the contras (→ 7).

MAY
Week 20 1987

Su	Mo	Tu	We	Th	Fr	Sa
					1	2
3	4	5	6	7	8	9
10	11	12	13	14	15	16
17	18	19	20	21	22	23
24	25	26	27	28	29	30
31						

10. Lyons: Klaus Barbie goes on trial for Nazi crimes (→ 7/4).

10. Lebanon: Beirut airport reopens after closing 98 days ago; tickets expensive due to soaring insurance rates (→ 6/1).

11. Washington: McFarlane, in testimony, links Reagan meeting with Saudi king to increase in Saudi aid to contras (→ 12).

11. New Delhi: India imposes direct rule on Punjab, accusing Sikh leaders of failing to quell violence (→ 16).

12. Washington: $10 mil. in contra aid from Sultan of Brunei said to have been put in wrong account by Col. North (→ 13).

12. Washington: Woody Allen and others testify in Congress against film colorization.

12. Manila: Aquino supporters win in vote for Senate (→ 7/27).

12. Jerusalem: P.M. Shamir calls For. Min. Peres' plan for peace talks "perverse" (→ 6/28).

12. U.S.: Last "Hill Street Blues" episode aired on NBC.

13. Washington: McFarlane tells panel he briefed Reagan often on contra supply efforts (→ 15).

13. Washington: Guatemalan president on first U.S. visit, asks Congress and president reconcile Central America policy.

13. Miami: Contras reorganize as Nicaraguan Resistance, elect seven-member board (→ 22).

14. Washington: Reagan rejects Salvadoran plea to let refugees live illegally in U.S. (→ 11/20).

14. Cairo: Egypt breaks diplomatic ties with Iran after attempt on life of ex-interior minister by fundamentalists.

14. Florida: Ralph Waldo Taylor, last American who fought at San Juan Hill, dies at 105.

15. Washington: Public Health Service urges mandatory AIDS tests for all seeking permanent residency in U.S. (→ 31).

16. Baltimore: Kentucky Derby winner Alysheba, Chris McCarron up, wins Preakness (→ 6/6).

16. New Delhi: Prime Minister Gandhi, in sharp attack on U.S., says West seeks to undermine India's democracy (→ 6/13).

Reagan says contra plan was "my idea"

"It was my idea to begin with."

May 15. President Reagan said today he was aware of private efforts to aid the Nicaraguan contras at a time when Congress had barred government aid to the rebel forces.

"I was very definitely involved in the decisions about support to the freedom fighters," he told a group of reporters at the White House. "It was my idea to begin with."

Until now, the president has claimed to have had only general knowledge of the private efforts to aid the contras. Robert C. McFarlane told congressional committees earlier this week he had briefed the president frequently on secret efforts to support the contras during the period Congress had cut off aid.

A White House official argued the president had not violated the law because the Boland amendment barring contra aid did not limit the president's conduct of foreign policy, an interpretation disputed by some members of Congress. McFarlane also maintained the president had not violated the law, but said Reagan "had a far more liberal interpretation" of the Boland amendment "than I did" (→ 17).

Near-misses are grave aviation problem

May 16. A major increase in near-collisions and air traffic control errors is a warning sign that the aviation safety system is in trouble, according to a number of experts.

The number of near-collisions, when aircraft come within 500 feet of each other in the air, rose from 311 in 1982 to over 600 last year, while operational errors by air traffic controllers increased by 18 percent in the past year.

The problems are blamed on a shortage of experienced air traffic controllers arising from the firing of illegal strikers in 1981, a lack of federal aircraft inspectors and lowered spending on maintenance by airlines feeling competitive pressures caused by deregulation.

Federal aviation officials say the system is basically sound, noting that there have been no fatal accidents involving major U.S. airlines this year. But they say they are recruiting new controllers, stepping up inspections and installing new safety devices at airports (→ 17).

Due to fate or incompetence, near-collisions are drawing the FAA's attention.

Beautiful Hayworth comes to a sad end

Hayworth's classic wartime pinup.

May 15. Rita Hayworth, the adored "Love Goddess" in more than 40 films, including "Gilda" and "Pal Joey," died yesterday in New York, 68 years old. Since 1981, she was under the care of her second daughter, Princess Yasmin, who, by publicizing her mother's tragic illness, drew attention to the then little known Alzheimer's disease. After years of deteriorating health, Miss Hayworth lapsed into a semicoma in February. The internationally famous screen temptress had been married to her manager Edward Judson (1937), Orson Welles (1943), Prince Aly Khan (1949), singer Dick Haymes (1953) and producer James Hill (1958).

Jesse Jackson leads in Democratic poll

May 16. The Rev. Jesse Jackson has emerged as a cautious favorite in the Democratic sweepstakes for the next presidential nomination, according to the latest New York Times/CBS poll. But while winning 17 percent support in the telephone survey, Jackson lagged behind when the polling was expanded to include some Democrats who have said they will not be candidates. The winner: Governor Mario Cuomo of New York, with a 25 percent favorable rating (→ 18).

Fiji army colonel seizes whole government

Fiji, in the South Pacific, is divided between ethnic Fijians and Indians.

May 14. There is trouble in paradise this evening. The newly elected civilian government of Fiji has been ousted in a military coup led by a colonel in the islands' army. Prime Minister Timoci Bavadra and members of his Cabinet are being detained at an unknown location. The airport is under military control, and telephone lines have been cut.

Trouble has been brewing in Fiji since elections were held last month. The islands' population is divided almost equally between ethnic Fijians and ethnic Indians. Almost all the members of the new government, however, are Indians. The colonel who led today's coup, Sitiveni Rabuka, is Fijian.

Rabuka is asking for recognition for his military government from Queen Elizabeth's representative on the island. Fiji is a member of the British Commonwealth (→ 19).

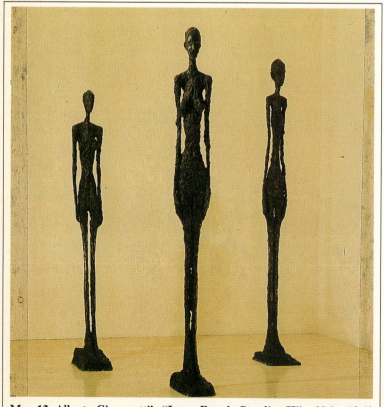

May 12. Alberto Giacometti's "Large Female Standing II" sold for $3.63 million today at Christie's in New York. It was a record for sculpture.

Dogs' health club is opened in Paris

Bowser getting a little flabby? Fido's arthritis flaring up? Two French doctors have just the cure. Dogform, a health club for dogs opened recently in Paris, provides one of the first opportunities for the canine community to participate in the health awareness boom. Doctors Friley and Forgeon have a competent staff of specialists, trained in physical therapy, massage and other techniques of sports medicine. They use lasers, sound waves, hot baths or whatever else it takes to bring your drooping dog back to his or her frolicking youth.

Reinvigorated, Spot may want to try competitive sports. For the aspiring athlete, the first Agility Dog championship was held last week. The contest consisted of a 140-yard obstacle course, complete with high hurdles, slalom and balance beam. It's guaranteed to separate the greyhounds from the poodles.

Soviet rocket is world's strongest

May 16. The Soviet Union has announced that it successfully tested a rocket powered by "the most powerful engines in the world today." The Energia, capable of putting 100 tons into orbit, was launched from the Baikonur Space Center in Kazakhstan, Soviet television said. It is propelled by eight liquid hydrogen engines that give it five times more weight-lifting capacity than the next most powerful Soviet launch vehicle.

American experts said the Soviet rocket engines probably are less powerful than those used on the Saturn 5, which sent Americans to the moon in the Apollo program. But the Saturn 5 has been out of production for many years. The Soviets thus have taken the lead in space propulsion after 20 years in second place.

The Energia stands 197 feet tall and has two stages. Its possible uses range from the launching of a Soviet space shuttle, believed to be under development, to the establishment of a large permanent space station to the launch of manned missions to other planets.

Meese Wedtech ties under investigation

Meese: Top lawyer broke the law?

May 11. A special prosecutor today took over a Justice Department investigation into whether Attorney General Edwin Meese 3rd violated any laws in his dealings with the Wedtech Corporation, a military contractor in the South Bronx. Meese said last month that when he was a presidential aide in 1982 he directed his staff to review Wedtech's efforts to obtain a $32 million contract with the Army. And three years later, Meese invested $60,000 with a financial consultant who worked with Wedtech but subsequently ended that business relationship.

$92m missing from Bakkers' PTL funds

May 15. Officials at the PTL ministry confirmed today that federal investigators want to have a look at their books. They are likely to find a lot of red ink. Accountants at the embattled ministry admit they cannot find $92 million. And that's not all. A 1939 Rolls Royce is also missing.

The accountants discovered the losses after Jim Bakker left his post as PTL Chairman in the middle of a sex and hush money scandal. Bakker has admitted having a relationship with a former church secretary, Jessica Hahn, who was later paid off to remain silent. A church official told reporters that federal officials have questions about "wire fraud, tax fraud and possible extortion" (→ 6/12).

Iraqi rocket strikes U.S. frigate Stark

The Persian Gulf has been the scene of battle between Iran and Iraq for nearly seven years, and is now an area of American involvement.

Draped in the stars and stripes, caskets in Bahrain await return to the U.S.

May 22. An Iraqi fighter plane zoomed above the USS Stark in the Persian Gulf five days ago and fired an Exocet missile from ten miles out. The warhead struck the ship's upper deck, sparking a blaze that burned into the hull. Thirty-seven American sailors were killed in the tragic attack.

The Pentagon believes that the warplane flew south from its base in Iraq along the Saudi coast, turned east, spotted the Stark, which was patrolling the Gulf's vital oil shipping lanes, and fired. The discovery of a second warhead, which lodged in the Stark but failed to explode, leads aviation experts to the conclusion that there were two Iraqi jets. A French-built Mirage F-1 can carry only one Exocet missile.

How could the Stark, with its sophisticated defense and radar equipment, fail to detect an Iraqi Mirage F-1's launching of a missile? According to the skipper of the Stark, Capt. Glenn Brindel, the ship's electronic warning device had not been activated. A crew member on lookout did identify the plane and issue a warning cry. But there had been no previous hostilities between Iraq and the U.S. in the Gulf, and so there was no reason to suspect an attack. U.S. Navy officials said that had an Iranian jet behaved in the same way, it would have been blasted from the sky.

Why did the Iraqi fighter plane attack? The Reagan administration feels the bombing was unintentional. Iraqi planes have fired on ships believed to be assisting its enemy, Iran, and there were such vessels in the general vicinity of the Stark. Today, President Reagan consoled the victims' families at an emotional memorial service (→ 6/6).

Simon, bow tie and all, joins in race

May 18. Senator Paul Simon of Illinois entered the race for the Democratic presidential nomination today, vowing to prove that his bow tie and his belief in traditional Democratic policies are not out of date. The former newspaper editor and author of 11 books announced his candidacy at Southern Illinois University in Carbondale. At age 58, he is the oldest in the field of contenders. "To become fashionable," Simon said, "some people tell me to get rid of my bow tie and my horn-rimmed glasses, and most of all to change my views." He noted that Harry Truman wore a bow tie and horn-rimmed glasses and never knuckled under to pressure to change his views on helping Americans (→ 6/9).

"Orient Express" is world poker champ

May 21. Every poker player dreams of drawing the card that will win him a million dollars, but it really happened for Johnny Chan, a China-born resident of Houston. When Chan drew a 9 of hearts for a pair, the 29-year-old restaurant owner won the 1987 World Championship of Poker and more than $1 million in cash and chips. Chan, known among poker players as the "Orient Express," outlasted a field of 152 starters who had put up $10,000 each. In the showdown, he beat an engineer who had bet $300,000 on a pair of 4's. The loser, Frank Henderson, had escaped bankruptcy several times during the week-long play, but was able to walk away with the second prize of $250,000.

Mozart manuscript sold for $4.34 mil.

May 22. A manuscript of nine Mozart symphonies set a new record for an auctioned musical manuscript today when it was sold after fierce bidding at Sotheby's in London for $4.34 million. The price eclipsed the previous such record of $548,000 set in 1983 by the first completed working draft of Stravinsky's "Rite of Spring," and only the Gospels of Henry the Lion, auctioned for $11.9 million in 1983, has ever fetched a higher manuscript price. Penned in the neat script of Mozart's Salzburg period, before he was 20 years old, the nine symphonies, numbers 22 to 30, were bought by an unidentified American and will be placed on deposit at the Pierpont Morgan Library in New York.

Garbage barge comes home, still loaded

The garbage barge, silhouetted by the New York skyline, returns unwanted.

May 18. The wandering garbage barge, a worldwide curio immortalized in song as the trash that nobody wanted, has returned home after a 60-day, 6,000-mile odyssey.

The barge, with 3,100 tons of fetid refuse piled atop it, and towed by a tug, has anchored off Brooklyn not far from Islip, Long Island, the little town where the quest for a final resting place started.

The garbage was turned away by six states and three countries before Islip agreed to take it back. But there is no place in Islip to unload it, and the barge sits quietly in New York Bay, as much a tourist attraction as the Statue of Liberty.

Paraphrasing a famous poem, the

mate of the tug Break of Dawn said, "Ours is not to question why. We just go where they tell us." They told the tug skipper to keep moving after being rejected by North Carolina, Alabama, Mississippi, Louisiana, Texas and Florida, as well as Mexico, Belize and the Bahamas.

New York Mayor Ed Koch said, "We are treating the garbage like Germany treated Lenin." He explained that "Lenin had to be in a sealed train" while passing through Germany on his return to Russia from Switzerland in 1917. In other words, he said, the garbage could pass through his city only if completely enclosed in sanitation trucks (→ 9/1).

Miniskirts are back, twenty years later

Knees are back as hemlines rise.

May 18. The mighty mini is here again, going from knee-skimmers to a full six inches up the thigh, resulting in a rush for knee-jobs at cosmetic surgeons' offices. The trouble with the mini? It is impossible to sit down. "Bring a coat," advise models. The good part? They make older women look sexy, since legs are the last part of the body to go. Some claim the miniskirt is a "social step, not a fashion trick." They state that women must try "to look happier and more playful in an increasingly tension-building world." Others quote Bette Davis regarding the short-short craze of the 60's. "In my day," she said, "hot pants were something we had, not wore."

"Ishtar," at $51m, looks like a flop

May 18. "Ishtar," after its first weekend out, has all of Hollywood thinking back to Michael Cimino's "Heaven's Gate," the industry's last bloated box office bust. The film, starring Warren Beatty and Dustin Hoffman, is five months late and $23 million over budget.

Reviewers have called it "colossally dunderheaded," "a runaway ego trip" and "a piffle with a $40-million-plus price tag." Box office returns have been no better: "Ishtar" made only $100,000 more than "The Gate," a horror film about some boys who find they can enter hell from their backyard. "The Gate," however, was made for one-twelfth the cost. Despite the problems, Elaine May's script -- about two sappy songwriters who stumble onto a CIA plot in a fictional Mideastern country—is clever and, at times, hilarious.

Myrdal, analyst of race relations, dies

May 17. Gunnar Myrdal, the Nobel Prize-winning Swedish economist and sociologist who left a lasting imprint on race relations in the United States, is dead at 88.

In 1944, Myrdal published his two-volume work, "An American Dilemma: The Negro Problem and Modern Democracy," in which he wrote that the conflict between American ideals and the reality of racism would be resolved in a reasonable time. The study was cited in a footnote in Brown v. Board of Education, the landmark Supreme Court ruling in 1954 that segregation in public schools was unconstitutional. "I've always been optimistic about America," he said. "Why? ... Because ideals mean something. They mean something special in America." Myrdal later became an outspoken critic of American policy in Vietnam.

Colorado devises plan to save wild horses

May 20. About 5,000 wild horses and burros may be killed to save money and grazing lands, according to a proposal by Bob Burford, Bureau of Land Management chief. "We destroy ten million excess dogs and cats each year," a spokesman for BLM said. "These surplus horses and burros are just as expensive to maintain." Thousands are rounded up each year from ten Western states and sold for $125 each. Although 70,000 have found

homes, it takes $9.3 million a year to keep the rest in facilities in Texas, Nebraska and Nevada.

Colorado has found a constructive way to help the situation: The state makes cowboys out of prisoners. Canon City Prison inmates are training 360 wild horses for adoption and use by the U.S. Forest Services. Though only one of the 28 inmates involved had previous horse experience, the program has proven successful.

In search of dry ground, wild horses swim across a swollen river.

MAY

Week 22 1987

Su	Mo	Tu	We	Th	Fr	Sa
					1	2
3	4	5	6	7	8	9
10	11	12	13	14	15	16
17	18	19	20	21	22	23
24	25	26	27	28	29	30
31						

24. S.F.: Golden Gate Bridge bends under weight of 250,000 revelers on its 50th anniversary.

25. Philadelphia: George Bush, Warren Burger, Mayor Wilson Goode mark bicentennial of Constitutional Convention.

25. Piscataway, N.J.: Johns Hopkins edges Cornell 11-10 to capture NCAA lacrosse title.

25. Washington: Voice of America says Soviets have stopped jamming broadcasts (→ 6/25).

25. Decatur, Ill.: Four girls barred from prom for wearing tuxedo jackets, leotards, tights.

26. Washington: William Webster sworn in as head of CIA.

26. Bucharest: Gorbachev, on Rumanian visit, gets cool response to speech on glasnost.

26. Washington: Supreme Court holds dangerous defendants may be held without bail.

26. Seattle: Liberal Archbishop Raymond Hunthausen gets post restored in compromise after clash with Vatican.

27. Brigham City, Utah: New space shuttle booster rocket passes first test.

28. Washington: Lewis Tambs, ex-ambassador to Costa Rica, says NSC, CIA, State Dept. ordered him to aid contras (→ 6/1).

28. Key West: Rafael del Pino Diaz, Cuban deputy chief of staff, defects to U.S. (→ 11/20).

28. U.S.: Allegis pays stockholders $60 per share, adding $3 bil. in debt to avoid hostile takeover.

28. Hatteras, N.C.: Deep-sea robot descends to recover USS Monitor, 1st armored battleship.

28. Washington: Stephanie Petit, 13, wins National Spelling Bee with "staphylococci."

29. L.A.: Director John Landis and four others cleared of three deaths on "Twilight Zone" set.

31. Washington: Reagan, in first speech exclusively on AIDS, calls for increased voluntary testing (→ 6/1).

DEATH

28. Charles Ludlam, rising leader in avant-garde theater, of AIDS (*4/12/1943).

German pilot, 19, lands in Red Square

May 30. Strollers in Moscow's Red Square were amazed when a small, single-engine plane set down in their midst yesterday, but Soviet officials were not amused.

As a result, Sergei L. Sokolov was relieved of his duties as Defense Minister and the military chiefs were rebuked for letting 19-year-old Matthias Rust of West Germany pilot his Cessna through heavily defended Soviet air space.

Rust, who flew the plane from Helsinki to Moscow, was hustled off for intensive questioning by the chagrined Russians. They wanted to know why their defense system could not detect the presence of a small plane that had penetrated more than 400 miles of their territory. The German teenager, with only 25 hours of flying time to his credit, managed to land the rented plane next to the Kremlin Wall at the foot of Red Square.

Matthias Rust, Kremlin in the background, cruises unhindered into Moscow.

The incident gave Soviet leader Mikhail Gorbachev the chance to replace Marshal Sokolov with a protege, Dmitri T. Yasov, as head of the Defense Ministry. The public castigation of the military was unusual; such things are usually handled behind the scenes (→ 9/4).

Al Unser wins Indy 500 for fourth time

May 24. Al Unser Sr., a hardbitten veteran of one of the most grueling of all sports, had to choke back the tears. He had just won the Indianapolis 500 auto race for the fourth time against all odds.

For one thing, at 48, he was the oldest ever to capture the grind. For another, he was a substitute driver, getting into the race when Danny Ongais was found unfit to drive after crashing in a practice round. In addition, Unser had not driven a car in competition all year because his boss, Roger Penske, decided to go with two instead of three drivers. "There were cars I could have driven but the ownership wasn't right," said Unser.

The happy ending: The elder Unser finished five seconds ahead of Roberto Guerro while his 25-year-old son, Al Jr., took fourth place. Unser Sr. tied A.J. Foyt for most Indy victories as 23 of the 33 starters failed to finish the race.

Just after the start of the race, Unser survived a close call, steering his number 25 around a skidding Josele Garza in the first turn.

Silicon Valley whiz kids bouncing back

May 25. After two years of hard times and a major shakeout, the Silicon Valley computer industry is making a major comeback.

A wide array of new products based on advanced technology has increased profits at many companies and put others back into the black. Sales of personal computers are booming, and so are markets for associated products, such as software. Profits are up 81 percent at Tandem Computers, 300 percent at Sun Microsystems and six percent at Apple Computer, despite heavy costs for introducing new models.

One factor driving the boom is the introduction of a new generation of microprocessors that give much more computing power at lower cost. Another is the availability of new software products designed to make use of the increased computing power. But there still are some clouds over Silicon Valley, a 50-mile stretch between San Jose and San Francisco. Chip manufacturers aren't making money because of heavy Japanese competition. And employment has not gone up, because the computer industry is wary of another downturn soon.

527-pound Hawaiian becomes Sumo star

Two thundering colossi test the ground as they prepare to do battle Sumo-style.

May 27. Few non-Japanese have ever invaded the almost mystical world of Sumo wrestling, which predates the Christian era as the national sport of Japan. Until now, with the raising of Salevaa Atisanoe of Hawaii to the level of ozeki, no non-Japanese ever achieved this honor as champion of the sport.

The 527-pound Hawaiian native broke with centuries of tradition by getting this signal honor from the Japan Sumo Association. Ozeki is only a rank behind the title of grand champion in Sumo's hierarchy.

There were tears in Atisanoe's eyes when he learned of the promotion. "I was practicing since yesterday what to say, but when I woke up this morning, my head was empty," said the former Hawaiian football player, who wrestles under the name of Konishiki.

Sumo wrestlers, with their enormous physiques, were part of ritualistic ceremonies for the Emperor. For more than 20 centuries, the sons of Sumo wrestlers were married to the daughters of Sumo wrestlers to perpetuate their enormous size. In a nation not noted for its height, the average Sumo offspring at maturity is 5 feet 9 inches and weighs 300 to 400 pounds.

Compact disc video introduced to public

May 30. Electronics buyers today got their first look at a revolutionary home entertainment product: the compact disc video, which holds 20 minutes of music with an accompanying video clip. North American Philips, which introduced the five-inch CD-V at the semi-annual Consumer Electronics Show in Chicago, says it could be as big as the music CD, which quickly captured a major share of the record market. A number of Japanese electronics companies will produce CD-V players and major American movie studios are planning to make CD-V's with digital sound.

Forbes throws party

May 28. If you were ever married to Mick Jagger or if your last name is Trump or if you're the chief of the CIA or a related organization, you were at Malcolm Forbes' bash today to celebrate the 70th anniversary of his magazine, Forbes. Twenty-eight helicopters took you to Forbes' 40-acre estate in New Jersey. Bagpipers and drummers, 140 of them, serenaded you. Pheasant and foie gras were served. Lasers and fireworks lit the sky. And a grand time was had by all.

Europe's Airbus is competitor for U.S.

May 30. Capturing 25 percent of world orders for jetliners, Airbus Industrie, a government-backed European consortium, is threatening United States dominance in the aircraft business. Airbus has recorded 440 orders for its 150-passenger, twin-jet A320 and is taking orders for two larger models that still are on the drawing board. The Boeing Company and McDonnell Douglas, the two American jetliner makers, say they are losing market share because Airbus is being unfairly subsidized by France, West Germany, Britain and Spain. Airbus says it's winning on merit.

Donovan acquitted

May 25. In what he called the end of a "nightmare," former Secretary of Labor Raymond J. Donovan was acquitted today of charges of fraud and grand larceny after an eight-month trial in the Bronx. The jury verdict was greeted by applause and cheers, with even jurors joining in the joyful scene. Donovan and his seven co-defendants, who also were cleared, were accused of a scheme to defraud the New York City Transit Authority of $7.4 million on a subway project.

May 31. Hockey fans in Edmonton have been treated to another Stanley Cup, their third in four years. Adding a tough defense to their renowned offense, the Oilers beat the Philadelphia Flyers four games to three.

May 26. Eddie Murphy's "Beverly Hills Cop II" has upset three records in its first weekend. One-day take: $9.7 mil.; three days: $26.3 mil.; screens: 2,326.

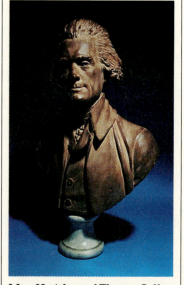

May 29. A bust of Thomas Jefferson, by Jean Antoine Houdon, was the model for the U.S. nickel. It brought $2.86 mil. today at Christie's, a record for portrait busts.

JUNE
Week 23 1987

Su	Mo	Tu	We	Th	Fr	Sa
	1	2	3	4	5	6
7	8	9	10	11	12	13
14	15	16	17	18	19	20
21	22	23	24	25	26	27
28	29	30				

1. Washington: Joe Fernandez, CIA chief in Costa Rica, says CIA chiefs at home knew of air drops to contras (→ 2).

1. U.S.: "Sgt. Pepper's Lonely Hearts Club Band" compact disk reaches stores exactly 20 years after original release.

1. Bonn: Chancellor Kohl's ruling coalition agrees to U.S.-Soviet plan to remove mid-range missiles from Europe (→ 7/22).

1. New York: Roy Williams, ex-Teamster chief, testifies Mafia controlled union (→ 9/8).

2. Washington: State Dept. aide Elliott Abrams admits "misleading" congressional panels on contra policy (→ 3).

2. Washington: State Dept. reports forged U.S. documents threaten U.S. foreign policy.

2. Amnesty International charges Cambodia with widespread use of arbitrary arrest and torture of political prisoners.

3. N.Y.: Rep. Mario Biaggi and five others indicted on Wedtech bribery charges (→ 9/22).

3. Washington: Albert Hakim says he set up $200,000 fund for personal use of Col. North (→ 8).

3. Washington: Rev. Leon Sullivan, author of Sullivan principles, calls for firms to pull out of South Africa (→ 7/18).

4. Madrid: Edwin Moses beaten by Danny Harris in 400-meter hurdles, ending record ten-year, 122-race streak.

4. N.Y.: Kidder, Peabody agrees to pay record $25.3 mil. to settle insider trading claims (→ 11/16).

5. Moscow: U.S. protests Soviet journal's claim that U.S. has gas that kills blacks and not whites.

5. N.Y.: Sri Lanka, at U.N., protests Indian support for Tamil rebels (→ 7/29).

6. Paris: Steffi Graf beats Martina Navratilova 6-4, 4-6, 8-6 for first Grand Slam title.

6. Washington: James K. Asselstine, leaving NRC after five years, calls nuclear plant safety levels perilously low.

6. Moscow: Deputy For. Min. Yuli M. Vorontsov says Soviets will not augment force in Persian Gulf despite U.S. plans (→ 9).

Gooden returns after drug suspension

A rehabilitated Gooden unleashes a high, hard fast ball against the Pirates.

June 6. There were 51,402 fans packed into Shea Stadium for a game one might think had World Series overtones. Instead, they were on hand for the return to action of Dwight Gooden, premier pitcher for the Mets, after his release from a drug rehabilitation program.

Making his first appearance since the 1986 World Series, Gooden pitched a four-hitter for six and two-thirds innings in racking up a 5-1 triumph over the Pittsburgh Pirates. He struck out five and walked four, earning a standing ovation. Before the game, no one could be sure how he would be received by the crowd.

Gooden had worked out regularly with the Mets since his release from a drug abuse center on April 29 after a 27-day stay. The 22-year-old right-hander admitted before the game that "I'm more nervous than when I pitched my first major-league game." One columnist had asked the fans to boo Gooden, but this did not materialize.

Segovia, who made guitar sing, is dead

Segovia made his debut in 1909, and was scheduled to tour when he died.

June 3. Andres Segovia, the virtuoso who restored the guitar to its revered status in the concert halls and conservatories of the world, died today of a heart attack at 94.

Born in southern Spain, Segovia gave undying devotion to the guitar at a time when it had long been ignored as a serious instrument. He was forced to study virtually on his own, against the objections of parents and teachers, and to rediscover works written for guitar in previous centuries. But his exhaustive studies paid off brilliantly. He became one of the master performers of the 20th Century, mesmerizing audiences and guitar disciples for decades and inspiring the major composers of his age to create new works for the instrument. He will be missed by millions of fans throughout the world.

Third international AIDS meeting held

June 1. More than 6,300 scientists and health workers met in Washington today at the Third International Conference on Acquired Immune Deficiency Syndrome, a week-long gathering on the deadly disease. The attendance was three times higher than the meeting's organizers had estimated, a measure of the concern felt by public health officials about the global impact of AIDS. The 51,000 cases reported in 112 countries are believed to be much lower than the real incidence, since many nations are reluctant to report AIDS cases; 36,000 cases have been reported in the U.S., and more than one million Americans are believed to be infected with the AIDS virus (→ 8).

Skeleton reopens debate on evolution

June 1. A 1.8-million-year-old fossil found in the Olduvai Gorge of Tanzania is changing scientific views about the path of human evolution. The fossil remains of an adult female of Homo habilis, the earliest true human species, were discovered last year by an expedition led by anthropologist Donald Johanson and are being shown for the first time this week.

The limb bones found by Johanson indicate that Homo habilis was much smaller than had been thought true of human ancestors, standing only 3.5-feet high. The skeleton also has more apelike features than had been expected, with long, heavy arms that dangled to the knees. It thus is much more like Australopithecus, the prehuman species that preceded it, than like Homo erectus, the next evolutionary step toward modern humans.

Until now, anthropologists assumed that progress toward erect stature and other human characteristics was slow but steady. It now appears that there was a rapid jump in evolution between Homo habilis and Homo erectus, which replaced it 200,000 years later. The question to be answered now is how did such a major transition from apelike to human features occur in what is an eyeblink in evolutionary terms.

Alan Greenspan replaces Volcker at Fed

Greenspan, new head of the Fed.

June 2. In a move that stunned the money markets today, President Reagan nominated Alan Greenspan to succeed Paul A. Volcker as the Chairman of the Federal Reserve Board, a job sometimes viewed as second only to the presidency in influence. While it appears unlikely that Greenspan will pursue a monetary policy markedly different from the course that has been taken by Volcker, bonds finished with one of the biggest losses on record and the dollar tumbled. Although Volcker had said in a letter to the president that he did not wish to be reappointed, it is believed he would have agreed to serve another term if the president had insisted.

Lebanon's Premier Karami is murdered

June 1. War-torn Lebanon suffered another shock today when Prime Minister Rashid Karami was killed by a blast, apparently from a bomb placed either beneath his seat or in his briefcase, while traveling in a military helicopter.

Karami, a Sunni Moslem, has recently been at loggerheads with President Gemayel, a Maronite Catholic, who opposed Karami's efforts to distribute power between Christians and Moslems. The Christian-dominated army is responsible for helicopter security, and fears of another civil war have arisen should Moslems blame Christians for the killing (→ 8/18).

Zoo's polar bears kill 11-year-old boy

It was meant to be a simple, mischievous adventure in Brooklyn's Prospect Park Zoo. For 11-year-old Juan Perez, it ended in tragedy. On a dare, he and two friends had hopped a fence after hours to cool off in the bear pond. Soon Juan was at the mercy of two 900-pound polar bears. "Go get help," he cried, "They're biting me hard." But by the time police arrived he was dead. The police, thinking more children could be trapped, shot the bears to death, drawing protest letters from hundreds of animal lovers. Mayor Ed Koch had a few explanatory words: Bears, he said, "are turf conscious, like human beings."

Roh nominated for Korean presidency

Ruling party nominee Roh Tae Woo.

June 2. Korean President Chun Doo Hwan selected Roh Tae Woo, a close associate and former army general, to be the ruling party's candidate to succeed him in the presidency. As the leader of the Democratic Justice Party, Chun was in a position to select his successor, and the party was expected to endorse his nomination later in the week. Chun has pledged to step down when his seven-year term expires in February, but there is still debate over the system to be followed in the election, which is expected in December. As a division commander, Roh moved his troops into Seoul to help Chun win power in a coup in 1979 (→ 10).

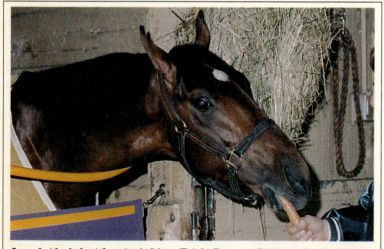

June 6. Alysheba (above) tried for a Triple Crown at Belmont. But Bet Twice, who placed second in the Preakness and Kentucky Derby, won by 14 lengths.

Wyeth's Helga pictures coolly received

June 1. Few events in the art world create as much excitement as the discovery of a secret cache of paintings by a well-known artist. Last summer, 240 portraits of a blonde model named Helga, secretly painted by Andrew Wyeth, were revealed, and a nationwide tour was booked. When the show opened last week, however, many critics took a dim view, saying Wyeth is an outstanding artist, but not a great one.

Helga, a local housekeeper, was Wyeth's artistic obsession for 15 years.

Su	Mo	Tu	We	Th	Fr	Sa
	1	2	3	4	5	6
7	8	9	10	11	12	13
14	15	16	17	18	19	20
21	22	23	24	25	26	27
28	29	30				

7. N.Y.: "Les Miserables" and "Fences" sweep Tony Awards.

7. Paris: Ivan Lendl tops Mats Wilander 7-5, 6-2, 3-6, 7-6 in final of French Open.

8. Washington: Atty. Gen. Edwin Meese orders AIDS tests for parole and immigration (→ 24).

8. Washington: Novice lawyer Bretton Sciarone, who failed bar four times, says he drafted legal opinion backing contra aid (→ 9).

8. Venice: Reagan at opening of economic summit, lifts economic sanctions on Japan (→ 8/31).

8. Cambridge: Derrick Bell, Harvard's first tenured black, begins sit-in at office to protest denial of tenure to two leftists.

9. Washington: Supreme Court rules government must compensate landowners for regulations which restrict use of land.

9. Venice: Summit conferees endorse principle of free shipping in Persian Gulf (→ 15).

9. Rutland, Vermont: Vietnam deserter Douglas Beane, 39, returns 18 years after going AWOL in Australia (→ 22).

10. Venice: Economic summit ends with only general plans.

10. Washington: U.S. to continue aid to Angola rebels (→ 9/9).

10. Wallops Island, Va.: Three NASA rockets accidentally launched by lightning.

11. Washington: Air traffic controllers vote new union, six years after Reagan broke strike.

11. "The Witches of Eastwick" opens, with Jack Nicholson.

11. Madrid: Socialists lose 21 big cities in Spanish vote.

12. Washington: U.S. drops spy charges against Corporal Arnold Bracy, second Marine accused in Soviet case (→ 8/21).

12. Central African Republic: Ex-Emperor Bokassa sentenced to death for at least 20 murders.

12. Fort Mill, S.C.: PTL ministry files for bankruptcy (→ 23).

13. Japan: Sachio Kinugasa breaks Lou Gehrig's 2,130-game record for consecutive games.

13. India: Sikhs kill 26 in New Delhi and Punjab (→ 7/6).

Fawn Hall tells all; states loyalty to North

Fawn Hall, loyal and dedicated, takes the oath before the congressional panel.

June 9. Fawn Hall gave new details today on how she helped Lieut. Col. Oliver L. North alter, shred and remove documents implicating him in the Iran-contra affair. In her second day before a congressional committee, the 27-year-old beauty and sometime model described the colonel as "every secretary's dream of a boss." She said she completely believed in him during his four years as a National Security Council aide.

"Sometimes," she said, "you just have to go above the written law."

Colonel North is the central figure in the probe into arms sales to Iran and diversion of funds to the contras in Nicarauga.

Miss Hall has testified that she altered some sensitive documents and destroyed others in a shredding machine. She also told of smuggling other key papers out of the office by hiding them under her clothing. On one occasion, she said, the colonel lent her $60 in traveler's checks, drawn on a Central American bank, that apparently had been given to him by Adolfo Calero, the contra leader. She said she repaid the loan a few days later (→ 23).

French government privatizing industry

June 7. France's Socialist experiment seems to be drawing to an end and many Frenchmen think its demise could not have come sooner. By the millions, they are withdrawing money from their savings accounts to invest in companies that are being denationalized and sold off by the government. Ten companies have already been purchased by private investors. Next week, one of France's largest banks, Societe Generale, will be up for grabs.

The privatization program has been dubbed "popular capitalism," and even opponents of Prime Minister Jacques Chirac's right-wing coalition admit it has been a resounding success. The program has its detractors, however. Critics claim that Finance Minister Edouard Balladur has deliberately undervalued stock in the companies for political reasons. Everyone agrees the prices have been attractive. Some of the offerings have been oversubscribed 65 times, and stocks have jumped 25% in value in less than a week.

Bess Myerson is named in scandal

June 10. A report commissioned by Mayor Koch has determined that Bess Myerson, former New York City Commissioner of Cultural Affairs, "improperly influenced" a judge who was presiding over the divorce case of her companion, Carl Capasso. It stated there was a "secret understanding" between her and Judge Hortense W. Gabel of State Supreme Court in Manhattan, whererby Ms. Myerson agreed to hire the judge's daughter as her special assistant at the Department of Cultural Affairs.

Two weeks after Ms. Gabel's hiring, Judge Gabel ordered Capasso's maintenance and child support payments reduced. The report also said Ms. Myerson failed to disclose "substantial" gifts from Capasso, a big city contractor. Ms. Myerson, a former Miss America, is a longtime friend of the mayor. And Mayor Koch says, "I continue to be a Bess Myerson friend. You have to forgive your friends" (→ 10/19).

Cicadas plague U.S.

June 7. An afternoon nap in the hammock may be all but impossible this summer in the Eastern United States once the periodic cicada appears for its brief but clamorous reign in the sunlight. The harmless insects, once mistaken for locusts, hibernate underground for 17 years before emerging by the billions for a mating ritual featuring a cacophonous song from the males. This year's strain is expected to be the largest ever seen.

Feebler KKK rallies

June 7. In marked contrast to earlier marches, Ku Klux Klan members staged a largely orderly parade through the streets of Greensboro, North Carolina, today. The 150 hooded and robed marchers were both cheered and taunted as they waved Confederate flags. Only five spectators were arrested on misdemeanor charges, and there were no injuries. In 1979, five leftist demonstrators were killed during a "Death to the Klan" rally in the same city (→ 18).

Thatcher wins new term

Thatcher-backers celebrate a resounding victory for England's middle class.

June 12. For the third time in a row, Margaret Thatcher has led her Conservative Party to a stunning electoral victory in England. The opposition Labor Party did manage to gain 21 seats in Parliament, but a record 13.7 million voters backed the Conservatives and they will have a majority of 100 seats in the House of Commons.

Prime Minister Thatcher's political program, dubbed "Thatcherism" by Fleet Street, has revolutionized British politics. It has also galvanized the middle class, which has emerged as a much more potent force than either the traditional aristocracy or the working class.

Under Mrs. Thatcher, millions of people from the middle class have bought homes and become stockholders. They showed their gratitude by voting for the Tories.

Labor leader Neil Kinnock says Mrs. Thatcher's supporters are only voting their selfish interests. He also says Mrs. Thatcher has ignored the millions of unemployed workers and sharpened the divisions between rich and poor. The prime minister disagrees. "Capitalism and enterprise," she says, "is a system which only works by spreading ever more widely to more and more of the population what used to be the privileges of the few."

Eric Staller was an architect and a photographer. Now he is known—at least in Coral Gables, Florida—as a sculptor. His "Lightmobile" is a 1967 VW with 1,659 computerized light bulbs that flash in 23 flowing patterns.

East Berlin youth riot, crying "Gorbachev"

June 9. For the last three nights, teenagers in West Berlin have been clapping their hands to the beat of Genesis, the English rock group. In East Berlin, young fans, separated from the sounds of the West by the Berlin Wall, clashed with police. Many of them yelled, "The wall must go." Others spat at officers, threw bottles and firecrackers and screamed, "Police pigs." From some of the demonstrators, there came an unexpected chant. "Gorbachev! Gorbachev!" they yelled.

East Berliners who live near the Brandenburg Gate say the demonstrations were the largest since a rock concert in East Berlin ten years ago. As calm returned to the streets this morning, many residents said they were surprised by the pro-Gorbachev sentiment.

To some of the young people in East Berlin, Gorbachev apparently represents a new style and departure, possibly even a new hope. The Soviet leader's call for glasnost, or openness, has struck a chord among students and intellectuals.

Political leaders in East Germany have been less impressed by Gorbachev's new policy. They have deleted any references to glasnost from Moscow reports. And today their spokesmen were denying that any demonstrations took place over the past three nights. "These exist only in the fantasy of foreign correspondents who drive over the border with the aim of creating sensations," the official East German news agency said.

Young West Berliners, envy of their Eastern peers, dance to live rock and roll.

Joe Biden makes presidential bid

June 9. Promising to rekindle the fire of idealism, Senator Joseph R. Biden Jr. of Delaware announced his candidacy for the Democratic nomination for president. In words reminiscent of those of the late President Kennedy, the 44-year-old senator made known his political ambitions in Wilmington, Delaware, the city where he once served on the county council before his election to the Senate in 1972. A skilled orator, the senator was applauded as he said: "For too long as a nation, we have been lulled by the anthem of self-interest," thus suffocating what he described as "the promise of America" (→ 29).

Big market earners average $68 million

June 9. Five researchers worked eight months to compile Financial World's list of Wall Street's biggest earners for 1986. The list, published in the current issue of the magazine, estimates that the average earnings of the ten best paid men on Wall Street was $68.7 million. The number one investor on the magazine's list was Michel David-Weill, senior partner of Lazard Freres & Co., who pulled down $125 million. Following him was George Soros, President of Soros Fund Management, with $90 to $100 million, and Richard Dennis of C&D Commodities, who earned $80 million last year.

Panama violence results in emergency

Riot police attempt to maintain control of the streets in Panama City.

June 11. A "state of urgency" has been declared in Panama in an attempt to restore order after four straight days of violent political protests. Civil and political rights have been curtailed in response to the worse crisis the Central American country has faced since the military takeover in 1968.

The protests were triggered by allegations made by Col. Roberto Diaz Herrera, until recently the second-highest ranking member of the Panama Defense Forces. Diaz has charged Panama's military leader, General Manuel Antonio Noriega, with fraud in the 1984 elections and with ordering the

murder in 1985 of Dr. Hugo Spadafora because of his criticism of the regime. These charges were not new, but Diaz supplied details that lent credence to the allegations.

The most shocking of Diaz's revelations concerned the 1981 death of Panama's leader, General Omar Torrijos Herrera, in a plane crash. The official investigation concluded that the crash was an accident, but Diaz claims that General Noriega had a bomb planted on the plane.

Noriega insists he will not resign, in spite of public calls for a return to democracy. The Reagan administration has been critical of the Panamanian government (→ 16).

Pope backs workers on visit to Poland

June 12. When workers leaving a papal mass in Gdansk, Poland, clashed with police, the Polish government was quick to point to the incident as an example of what can happen when "political provocateurs ... exploit religious occasions to air" unsocialist ideas. The disturbance began when a cordon of helmeted riot police blocked a group of 15,000 people. The Pope's homily was centered on the theme of Polish Solidarity, both as a concept and as an organization, and the site of the mass was near the home of Lech Walesa, leader of the worker's rights movement in that country.

Last "Prairie Home Companion" heard

June 13. We will hear no more of the women who are strong, the men who are good looking and all the children who are above average. "A Prairie Home Companion," public radio's most popular program, signed off tonight after 13 years on the air. Its host and creator, Garrison Keillor, feels he has exhausted his sources of homespun humor and small-town philosophy. The show emanated from fictional Lake Wobegon, an earnest Minnesota hamlet where the term social disease referred to boisterousness. Doings in the retiring town can be followed on into 1988 as reruns are broadcast.

Korean violence worsens

June 10. Seoul was rocked by the worst street violence in years as anti-government protesters fought for hours with riot police. At times, the protesters, mostly students, were in control of the streets, with police retreating until reinforcements could arrive. Streets in central Seoul were littered with stones thrown by the protesters and reeked of tear gas fired by police.

The government reported that demonstrations were held in at least 11 other cities in Korea and that more than 2,000 persons had been arrested nationwide.

The protests overshadowed a gala reception by President Chun Doo Hwan and his ruling Democratic Justice Party to celebrate the

Anger in the streets of Seoul.

selection of Roh Tae Woo as the party's candidate for president. Roh is virtually certain to be elected under an electoral college system challenged by the opposition (→ 15).

Reagan asks Berlin Wall be torn down

June 12. President Reagan went to the Berlin Wall today and challenged Soviet leader Mikhail Gorbachev to tear it down, to prove he is really a man of peace.

The president spoke just 100 yards from the wall, which the Communists built in 1961 to shut off an exodus of East Germans to the West. He was heard by 20,000 people, including U.S. military personnel and their families. Police kept hostile demonstrators away.

Before he spoke, Reagan peered from the old Reichstag Building into East Berlin, across the wall, and said, "I think it's an ugly scar."

The president said NATO's deployment of Pershing-2 and cruise missiles had successfully countered the threatening Soviet deployment of SS-20's, and thus made possible the negotiated elimination of all such medium-range missiles.

His speech at the wall recalled similar earlier appearances by Presidents Kennedy and Carter. American presidents come to Berlin, Reagan said, "because it is our duty to speak in this place of freedom."

The day before President Reagan arrived, 24,000 leftist demonstrators clashed with police in the streets of West Berlin. But some leftists opposed anti-Reagan demonstrations while he was negotiating with the Soviets.

Geraldine Page, fine actress, dies

June 13. Geraldine Page has died of a heart attack in New York. She was 62. The news shocked and saddened cast members of "Blithe Spirit," the Broadway play she had been performing in since spring.

Miss Page recently won an Oscar for her portrayal of a nostalgic Texan in the film "The Trip to Bountiful." Moviegoers wondered where Miss Page had been hiding herself; the screen was rarely treated to her talents. Her home was the stage, in plays like Tennessee Williams' "Summer and Smoke" and "Sweet Bird of Youth." There she could best display her tender complexity.

An Oscar for "A Trip to Bountiful."

JUNE
Week 25 1987

Su	Mo	Tu	We	Th	Fr	Sa
	1	2	3	4	5	6
7	8	9	10	11	12	13
14	15	16	17	18	19	20
21	22	23	24	25	26	27
28	29	30				

14. Bonn: Willy Brandt, 73, formally steps down as head of Social Democrats after 20 years.

15. U.S.: Supreme Court bars evidence of victim's suffering at death sentence hearings.

15. Atlantic City, N.J.: Michael Spinks scores fifth-round knockout over Gerry Cooney.

15. Seoul: Tens of thousands take to streets; U.S. disavows immediate diplomatic initiative (→ 24).

15. Washington: Reagan justifies role in Persian Gulf as defense against Soviets (→ 16).

16. U.S.: Justice Dept. calls special prosecutor law illegal.

16. Panama: Stores reopen as street violence recedes (→ 7/1).

16. Orlando, Fla.: Last dusky seaside sparrow dies, seventh bird type to die off in U.S.

17. Denver: Federico Pena, city's first Hispanic mayor, wins re-election in comeback victory.

17. Washington: FAA test of airlines' security finds 20% of weapons went undetected (→ 7/28).

18. Arizona: Gov. Mecham, under fire for rescinding Martin Luther King Holiday, calls "day of recognition" for King (→ 9/8).

18. Washington: Researchers report first definitive evidence that reducing cholesterol will deter clots in arteries.

18. Beirut: U.S. journalist Charles Glass kidnapped in Shiite suburb with son of Lebanese defense minister (→ 8/18).

18. Hanoi: Prime Minister Pham Van Dong and President Truong Chinh, last of Ho Chi Minh's colleagues, ousted by National Assembly.

19. Washington: Capt. Glenn R. Brindel, Stark commander, relieved of duty (→ 7/20).

20. Washington: Reagan vetoes broadcast fairness legislation.

20. Washington: N.Y. Times reports Saudis gave billions in aid over last 15 years to U.S.-backed anti-Marxist groups.

20. Nassau: Lynden O. Pindling wins sixth term as premier, playing on fears of U.S. domination.

Seoul police lose control

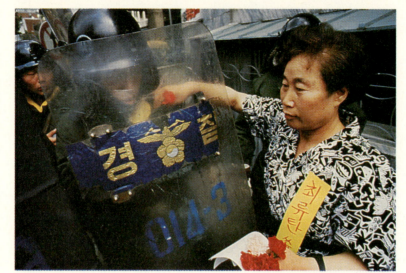

Shades of the sixties: A Korean woman hands flowers to riot police.

June 20. A surge of violence, marked by street fighting between students and police, swept through South Korea, plunging the country into a serious political crisis.

After ten days of mounting demonstrations in Seoul and other major cities, the government warned it would take extraordinary measures to stop the unrest, but there was growing doubt it could contain it short of making concessions.

In Seoul at one point, police lost control of the streets as tens of thousands of students tore through the city, throwing rocks and gasoline bombs. In a square before the Bank of Korea, the students overwhelmed police, stripping them of their gas masks and riot gear.

There were indications that the protest was spreading beyond the students to the middle class. About 10,000 persons held a candle-light vigil outside the Myongdong Cathedral in downtown Seoul, singing songs of protest. The tension has been mounting ever since President Chun ruled out the direct election of a president (→ 24).

June 14. Kareem Abdul Jabbar, a balding basketball wonder at 40, helped the L.A. Lakers close out the NBA finals over Boston with 32 points, and win their 4th title in 8 years. Magic Johnson was Most Valuable Player.

U.S. Gulf patrol on hair-trigger alert

June 16. American sailors are manning battle stations, ready to attack if any aggressor threatens U.S. ships in the Persian Gulf. Top Pentagon officials have issued the hair-trigger alert to avoid another attack like the one last month on the USS Stark. The alert was also declared to allay congressional concerns about the Reagan administration's controversial Persian Gulf policy. Currently, U.S. ships are escorting Kuwaiti tankers, which some congressional leaders feel is an unnecessary mission. Another attack on a U.S. ship would result in immediate reprisal. Senator Alan Cranston said, if a strike occurs, "we are at war" (→ 19).

Bus line buys rival

June 19. Greyhound bus lines today announced plans to buy Trailways, its chief competitor, for $80 million. Greyhound will continue to serve the 1,200 communities reached by the rival company and will buy many of Trailways' buses. The fate of 4,000 Trailways employees, however, is uncertain. Analysts blame a recent slump in Trailways business on cheaper air fares.

Ford is divesting

June 14. The Ford Motor Company, in a somewhat surprising move, has decided to sell its interests in South Africa. Although negotiations have been taking place for months, Ford Chairman Donald E. Petersen said last month that Ford did not want to leave South Africa. Ford owns 42 percent of its subsidiary, the South African Motor Corporation, or Samcor, and the Anglo American Corporation owns the rest.

Ford proposes to put more than half of its shares into a trust for its workers, 70 percent of whom are black, and sell the remainder to Anglo American. Ford would not completely sever its ties to South Africa; it will still sell components to Samcor. Over 100 companies have left South Africa since 1984 to protest apartheid.

Goetz guilty of gun charge, but not murder

Despite white faces in this protest, the verdict has split N.Y. along racial lines.

June 17. A jury has acquitted Bernhard Goetz of twelve counts stemming from the December 22, 1984, incident in which Goetz shot four teenagers who, he claimed, were attempting to rob him.

Acquitted of, among other charges, attempted murder, assault and reckless endangerment, Goetz was nevertheless convicted on the charge of illegal weapons possession. The single conviction is a Class D felony and could carry a sentence of up to seven years, although the judge, Justice Stephen G. Crane, is under no obligation to impose any sentence at all.

According to testimony, Goetz pulled his unlicensed weapon on the four teenagers when one of them demanded five dollars from him. The defense maintained that Goetz, who had been mugged and beaten in 1981, had heightened intuition about threats and body language and knew that the youths intended to rob him. Civil-rights advocates suggest that if the teenagers had not been black, the trial may have had another outcome.

Carson weds again

June 20. "Tonight Show" host Johnny Carson, 61, has said "I do" for the fourth time. Though he has cited his devotion to work as the stumbling blocks thrice before, former legal secretary Alexis Maas, about 35, whom he met a year ago, has made him dare to try again.

Johnny and 35-year-old Alexis.

Creation law voided

June 19. In a seven-to-two vote, the Supreme Court has dealt a blow to the efforts of fundamentalist Christians to influence public school curricula. The issue at hand was a 1981 Louisiana law that required public schools to teach creationism as science, along with the theory of evolution. Justice William J. Brennan Jr., speaking for the court, said that the law was unconstitutional because "the preeminent purpose of the Louisiana Legislature was clearly to advance the religious viewpoint that a supernatural being created humankind."

The two dissenting Supreme Court Justices, Antonin Scalia and William Rehnquist, called the decision "repressive," saying the ruling denied the people of Louisiana "whatever scientific evidence there may be against evolution" (→ 8/26).

JUNE
Week 26-27 1987

Su	Mo	Tu	We	Th	Fr	Sa
	1	2	3	4	5	6
7	8	9	10	11	12	13
14	15	16	17	18	19	20
21	22	23	24	25	26	27
28	29	30				

21. San Francisco: Scott Simpson wins U.S. Open by one stroke over Tom Watson.

22. N.Y.: Tom Seaver, 41, ends 16-day comeback with Mets.

22. U.S.: Whitney Houston, with "Whitney," becomes first woman to have album debut at #1.

22. Chile: Protesters riot over killing of 12 alleged leftists by govt. agents last week (→ 8/13).

22. San Juan, Puerto Rico: Two get 99 years, one 75 years in Dupont Plaza hotel fire.

22. Quantico, Va.: Douglas Beane, Vietnam deserter, gets discharge, not court-martial.

23. Washington: Ex-CIA agent Glenn Robinette testifies North used Iran arms sale funds to pay for home security system (→ 25).

24. Seoul: Opposition leader Kim Young Sam, in meeting with President Chun, rejects plan for compromise (→ 25).

24. Bonn: West Germany says it will try alleged terrorist Mohammed Ali Hamadei in Bonn.

24. Geneva: UNICEF chief in Belgium resigns over scandal tying organization to child pornography ring.

25. Washington: Supreme Court rules military personnel may not sue superiors or government.

25. Washington: Asst. Atty. Gen. Charles Cooper names Casey, North and Poindexter in Iran-contra cover-up (→ 7/7).

25. Seoul: Kim Dae Jung released from house arrest (→ 29).

26. U.S.: Stanley Kubrick's "Full Metal Jacket" opens.

27. Washington: Four-day-old panda cub dies; would have been first to be raised in U.S.

29. Seoul: President Chun agrees to opposition demands for direct presidential elections (→ 7/1).

30. N.Y.: Bolshoi Ballet opens U.S. tour at Metropolitan Opera.

30. Haiti: Nationwide strike in second day of protest against military government's seizure of electoral process (→ 7/2).

30. Cleveland: United Church of Christ is first major Protestant church to affirm validity of Judaism.

Four fliers break round-world record

June 21. Four fliers have successfully completed a round-the-world flight that parallels the 1938 journey made by the late Howard Hughes in a twin-propeller plane. They lowered the record set by Hughes by two and a half hours, completing the 14,640-mile trip in 88 hours and 48 minutes.

"We did it, it's over and I am a happy man," said one of the four, Arthur Powell of Vancouver. They found a replica of the 1930's plane used by Hughes in Miami, where it was being used to transport chickens, according to the plane's captain, Patrick Forti. The fliers had to bypass the Soviet Union when the Kremlin refused permission.

Who's that girl in Japan? Madonna!

June 29. Pop star Madonna previewed her songs and sleeker, blonder look in Japan this month with resounding success. Worshipping fans, some of whom paid scalpers up to $700, marveled at an elaborate stage spectacular featuring seven costume changes and eight giant video screens to project the image of their idol. The show is now headed for a tour of North American arenas to coincide with her new album and movie, both called "Who's that Girl?" But husband Sean Penn, the actor with the penchant for fisticuffs, won't be seen with Madonna. He's been sentenced to begin two months in jail.

Madonna plays Tokyo.

Pope John Paul II meets Kurt Waldheim

Waldheim (seated) and the Pope.

June 25. In spite of widespread protests by world Jewish organizations and the marked absence of United States diplomats, Pope John Paul II met today with Kurt Wald-heim, President of Austria.

Waldheim formerly Secretary General of the United Nations, was implicated in the deportation of Greek Jews to Nazi death camps during World War II. In his public remarks, following a 35-minute private meeting with Waldheim, the pope made no mention of the Austrian's wartime record.

Israeli Prime Minister Yitzhak Shamir commented on the meeting, saying, "It could be interpreted as a justification for crimes of which Waldheim is accused." Other Jewish organizations staged protests at the Vatican and in Washington. Ambassadors from the United States were conspicuously absent from the ceremony in which the pope welcomed Waldheim. The Vatican has issued several statements claiming the Austrian president was welcomed as a head of state, not as an individual (→ 9/1).

Bakker offers apology to Jessica Hahn

June 23. Jim Bakker, the fallen preacher, says he is sorry. In an exclusive interview with USA Today, the former head of the PTL offered an apology to Jessica Hahn for the tryst that led to his ouster from the ministry. "It was a terrible mistake," Bakker said, "and I believe Christ has forgiven me." Bakker denied knowing that hush money had been paid to Hahn.

Looking weak and exhausted, Bakker also said he will "not throw mud" at the Rev. Jerry Falwell, the new PTL chief. As a peace gesture, Bakker said he will move out of his PTL home in South Carolina. He is also promising a comeback. Bakker says he has been invited "to the great pulpits of America" (→ 11/15).

Hahn: Shot into the spotlight.

Radio "shock jocks" ignore new guidelines

June 21. It has been two months since the Federal Communications Commission issued new guidelines to curb what it considers indecent radio programming. But a recent survey conducted by USA Today of seven popular "shock jock" programs, as they're called, has revealed that few of these have cleaned up their act. Obscene language still reigns on these shows.

The FCC guidelines are intended to eliminate material "that depicts or describes, in terms patently offensive as measured by contemporary community standards for the broadcast medium, sexual or excretory activities or organs."

The "shock jocks" monitored include Jim Trenton of KROQ in Los Angeles and Howard Stern of WXRK in New York.

Gorbachev urges economic restructuring

June 25. Soviet leader Mikhail Gorbachev ignored internal criticism of his policies today as he boldly advocated the most sweeping changes in the Soviet economy since the days of Stalin. Gorbachev said it is time to start phasing out price subsidies and central economic controls. He made his proposals in a speech to the Communist Party's Central Committee.

Under the Soviet system, the prices of hundreds of thousands of items are set by the central government. In his speech today, Gorbachev did not pull any punches as he said the system is not working. "Comrades," he said, "we cannot put up with the lag in community and consumer services, with an unsatisfactory situation in passenger transport, communications, tourism, physical training and sport."

The key element in the new plan is a reduction in the influence of several powerful, centralized agencies. Instead of managing intricate details of the Soviet economy, they will only set general guidelines.

A Soviet specialist who has criticized previous Gorbachev reforms as inadequate said he is surprised by the plan. Ed Hewitt, an expert with the Brookings Institution, told The New York Times in Moscow, "I can't complain any longer that he isn't talking about radical reform" (→ 8/24).

Ordinary Joe gets British royal title

The Earl of Wharncliffe now runs a construction crew. In Cumberland, Maine, they still call him Rick. But Richard Wortley, 34, has inherited the title of his father's cousin, who died last week in England. He could take a seat in the House of Lords, or relax on his 4,800-acre estate in Yorkshire. But Rick insists, "I'm an American and I'm going to stay that way." According to an editor of "Debrett's Peerage," "He is already the earl, whether he likes it or not." But he can renounce the title.

Swede breaks world high jump record

June 30. With a hometown crowd cheering him on, Patrik Sjoberg soared 7 feet, 11.25 inches to a new world high jump record at a Grand Prix track and field meet in Stockholm. Hundreds of fans spilled onto the track as the happy Swede ran a victory lap. This was the final event of the day, but most of the 20,000 fans were still on hand, waving Swedish flags. Sjoberg surpassed the world record of 7 feet, 10.75 inches set by Igor Paklin of the Soviet Union at the World University Games in Japan in 1985.

Orthodox Jews battle secularism in Israel

June 28. According to Daniel J. Elazar, an expert on religious politics, "a serious Jewish fundamentalist revival is gaining strength in Israel." Israel's religious melting pot simmers with four distinct groups and various smaller sects. While most Israelis are Zionists, attention has lately focused on the non-Zionist Haredim, or "ultra-Orthodox," who account for only five percent of the population. Their influence is growing as they hold the balance of power in the Knesset. In their opinion, modern Israel is an "evil" society, and they have begun to put many secular Israelis on the defensive with their appeals to close movie houses and ban sexually suggestive ads from bus stops (→ 7/8).

Orthodox Jews protest in Jerusalem.

John Huston, one of the movie greats, dies

Huston, still directing at 81, on the set of "Under the Volcano" (1984).

Aug 28. An indomitable force in movie making, John Huston, has died in Rhode Island at the age of 81. Huston suffered from emphysema for several years, but worked on; he was in Rhode Island for the filming of his latest picture, to be based on a Thornton Wilder novel.

Huston often based his films on popular books, but they rarely had a bookish feel. "The Maltese Falcon" (1941), his directorial debut, was a brilliant translation of Dashiell Hammett's mystery tale. The mild short story "The African Queen" (1950) became a rollicking, boisterous movie in his hands.

The 6-foot-2 Huston couldn't help but be a towering presence; when he cast his father, Walter, in "The Treasure of the Sierra Madre," it seemed almost natural for the more diminutive father to take direction from his son. His own children found it hard to emerge from his shadow; daughter Anjelica held back from acting in one of his films until "Prizzi's Honor" came along. She won an Oscar, just like her grandpa in "Treasure."

Huston walked away from a few near-fatal accidents, risked his life in big-game hunts, gambled, boxed and wed five times. "One must avoid personal cliches," he once said. That restlessness was reflected in his films—an unpredictable style with predictable excellence.

Trudeau opposes new Canadian pact

Aug 28. Pierre Elliott Trudeau returned to Parliament in Canada today, this time to testify against a proposed new constitutional pact that would give the provinces some powers now held by the central government. In the three years since ending his 15-year tenure as Prime Minister, Trudeau had all but disappeared from public view. Well aware of this, he said, with a touch of sarcasm, "Maybe I am passe. Maybe there is a new Canada now." During his two and a half hours of testimony, he proved to be a bit of a sensation, alternately scathing, witty and intellectually imperious. "Like old times, huh?" he quipped as he entered the room.

Kohl joins in plan to scrap missiles

Aug 26. Chancellor Helmut Kohl opened the way to an American-Soviet treaty that would limit medium- and short-range missiles when he said West Germany would scrap its Pershing 1A missiles if the two superpowers reached an agreement. Accord on an intermediate-range missile treaty was imperiled when the Soviets insisted that West Germany's 72 Pershings would have to be included. Kohl balked at that request but said he would voluntarily dismantle the Pershings because, "I want to help the American President to successfully conclude the Geneva talks." A pact to rid Europe of shorter-range missiles is expected (→ 9/2).

Japan still setting fast competitive pace

Aug 31. A middle-aged American turns to his wife and says: "The Japanese have already surpassed us in compact discs, and I don't even know what they are." The cartoon sums up an inescapable fact: Japan is now the leading manufacturing nation and the richest society on earth.

The Japanese, with eight of the ten largest banks, control the world banking system. Japanese trading profits are the world's largest, and the country is the world's biggest net creditor. Japan has conquered world markets in textiles, televisions, steel, autos and semiconductors. The world's richest man is Japanese (real estate baron Yiosiaki Tsutsumi is worth $21 billion). One Japanese golf club costs $2 million to join. And 80 percent of Japanese consider themselves middle class.

How did it all happen? The Japanese are hard-working, thrifty and highly organized. Social cohesion (they operate by a family-like consensus) and egalitarianism are also factors. The result is a society that combines the low labor costs of a developing nation with the high productivity of a developed one.

Dow, up 25.35, sets record of 2,722.42

Aug 25. It is almost Labor Day, but stock investors have not taken their summer vacations yet. The market is still boiling over in the August heat, and the bulls are running up a sweat. The Dow Jones industrial average jumped more than 25 points yesterday, closing above 2,722. That is another record, if you are still counting. The Dow has soared almost 2,000 points in the past five years. The latest statistics from Washington gave the market a shot in the arm. Orders for factory equipment and non-defense capital goods were up a very strong 1.6 percent (→ 9/4).

Rustin, civil rights advocate, succumbs

Aug 24. Following surgery for a perforated appendix and peritonitis, pacifist and civil rights activist Bayard Rustin died today at the age of 75. Rustin is best known for his efforts in planning the 1963 March on Washington for Jobs and Freedom, the mass demonstration where Martin Luther King Jr. gave his "I have a dream" speech. It paved the way for the civil rights bills of 1964 and 1965. A tireless organizer, Rustin was a firm believer in non-violent tactics, democratic procedures and the knowledge that all people are one. He was admired as a political philosopher.

Japanese families walk on the Ginza, Tokyo's Times Square. Neon and thriving retail businesses are some of the special effects of Japan's economic miracle.

Su	Mo	Tu	We	Th	Fr	Sa
		1	2	3	4	5
6	7	8	9	10	11	12
13	14	15	16	17	18	19
20	21	22	23	24	25	26
27	28	29	30			

1. Washington: Inquiry reveals CIA workers profited from sale of rare agency-bought stamps.

1. California: Protester Brian Wilson has legs severed by train carrying arms to Concord Naval Weapons Station.

1. Washington: FDA approves lovastatin, new drug for lowering cholesterol.

1. Johannesburg: Two blacks hanged for murder in first executions since eruption of turmoil in Sept. 1984 (→ 20).

1. Brooklyn: Incineration begins for 3,100 tons of waste from garbage barge, rejected by three countries and six states.

2. Oskarovka, U.S.S.R.: Private team of U.S. and Soviet scientists monitors blast to prove verifiability of nuclear test ban (→ 5).

2. Persian Gulf: Eight ships hit by Iraqi planes and Iranian vessels in most concentrated attack of war (→ 21).

2. U.S.: People meters make debut in attempt to find new way of monitoring TV viewing.

3. Burundi: Leftist Pres. Jean-Baptiste Bagaza overthrown by military while in Quebec for French-speaking summit (→ 5).

3. Islamabad: Pakistani parties, in rare display of unity, denounce U.S. pressure for data on nuclear capabilities (→ 29).

3. Washington: Study finds vets who served in Vietnam have higher death rate from cancer.

4. Washington: Federal Reserve hikes discount rate from 5.5% to 6% in attempt to stall inflation; first hike in three years (→ 11).

4. Ulsan, South Korea: Police arrest 200 strikers in biggest roundup in two months of labor strife (→ 14).

4. Washington: U.S. decides to continue aid to Haiti despite killing of more than 25 protesters this summer (→ 10/13).

5. Seattle: Libertarians choose Ron Paul, Texas ex-congressman, for presidential race (→ 7).

5. New York: John McEnroe fined $7,500 for outburst during first round of U.S. Open.

5. Lebanon: Israeli air raid kills 41 in south (→ 11/14).

U.S. legislators inspect Soviet radar base

Sept. 5. In a dramatic example of its open, or savvy, new approach toward foreign policy, the Soviet Union has allowed a congressional delegation to tour the top-secret and controversial Krasnoyarsk radar facility in Siberia.

The purpose of the giant radar station has been a subject of intense debate among arms control experts since the Krasnoyarsk radar was discovered by American spy satellites four years ago. The Reagan administration claims that the radar violates the 1972 Anti-Ballistic Missile Treaty because it is designed to track approaching enemy missiles. The Soviets say the radar is for tracking satellites in orbit.

The four-hour tour defused some, though not all, of the suspicions of the delegation, which included three Congressmen and four aides specializing in military affairs. The radar did not appear protected enough to be used in the event of a nuclear war. At the same time, it did not appear directed correctly if its sole purpose was to monitor satellites (→ 18).

Jews discuss Waldheim visit with Pope

Italian Jews greeted Waldheim in Rome with stark reminders of the Holocaust.

Sept. 1. In a rare meeting with Jewish leaders, Pope John Paul II faced criticism about his recent meeting with Kurt Waldheim, the President of Austria, who has been implicated in the deportation of Greek Jews to Nazi death camps during World War II. Although the pope offered no direct response to the anger of Jews, and there was no resulting change in Vatican policy concerning the state of Israel, today's meeting has served to defuse a potentially volatile situation. Following the audience, the Vatican announced that it would soon release a document clarifying Church policy on the Holocaust as well as other aspects of anti-Semitism.

First known case: Researcher gets AIDS

Sept. 4. The first known case in which a laboratory worker was infected with the AIDS virus by working with it was reported today by the National Cancer Institute. The worker and the laboratory were not identified, and federal officials said they were unsure whether violations of safety regulations led to the infection. Laboratory workers are required to wear gloves and take other precautions when handling the deadly virus. Several health workers have been infected when they stuck themselves with needles or made similar mistakes while working with blood from AIDS patients, but no one involved with AIDS research has been infected in the laboratory until now (→ 10/2).

90th execution held since 1976 decision

Sept. 1. The robbery netted William Mitchell $160, but cost him his life. While holding up a Georgia grocery store, Mitchell shot and killed a 14-year-old boy. He was sentenced to death for the crime and has become the 11th person executed in the state since Georgia resumed the death penalty in 1983 and the 90th execution nationwide since the 1976 U.S. Supreme Court ruling which allowed states to reinstate capital punishment.

Exhibition honors long-exiled Chagall

Sept. 2. Marc Chagall certainly gave the Soviet Union a chance. The artist, who died in March 1985 in Paris, lived for 97 years—more than enough time for the U.S.S.R. to make up for its neglect of the master painter's work. But the Soviets choose to time honors for expatriates carefully; that is, posthumously. An exhibition of Chagall's work finally opened today at the Pushkin Museum in Moscow.

More than 250 prints, paintings and drawings are on display, culled from private collections and from national museum storerooms. The painting "The Stroll" (1917-18) seems the unintentional centerpiece of the exhibition. Visitors stop to take a long look at the image of Chagall and his young wife floating high in the clouds, at ease and beyond reach.

Marc Chagall (above) died in 1985.

Chad forces destroy major base in Libya

Chadians graphically demonstrate the desire to keep their country united.

Sept 5. Chadian forces have reportedly destroyed the Matan as Sarra air base in southeastern Libya, which was used to launch bombing missions against Chad. This is the first time that Chadian troops have attacked a target in undisputed Libyan territory.

Chad's army ousted the Libyans in a military offensive that ended with the capture of the Aouzou Strip, located along the two countries' border. Libya, which recaptured Aouzou August 28, claims the territory, but it is internationally recognized as Chadian.

Libya has at different times backed each of the two main contenders for power in Chad's long-running civil war, Hissen Habre, Chad's current President, and Goukouni Oueddei.

Francophone nations end Quebec summit

Sept 5. Leaders of 41 French-speaking nations and territories today adjourned a three-day summit meeting in Quebec. They expressed the hope that the group, called La Francophonie, will have as effective a world role as the British Commonwealth. Formally established in Paris 18 months ago, the organization will meet again in Dakar, Senegal, in 1989, and stage a sports festival in Morocco the same year.

One problem among members is the distaste some have for the human rights records of others. "La Francophonie is definitely raising the issue, but you must give it time," said French President Francois Mitterrand. "We're not here to organize a collective police force."

Leaders of the world's French-speaking nations in conference in Quebec.

Young German flier sent to Soviet camp

Sept 4. The prosecutor asked for an eight-year jail term, but the 19-year-old German who flew a light plane into Red Square last May, was sentenced to four years in a Soviet labor camp. Matthias Rust, arrested after violating Soviet air space with his flight from Helsinki, accepted his punishment stoically. "I was prepared for it," he said. One witness, an aviation expert, said Rust had wandered into Moscow commercial flight lanes on his 4,000-mile trip. The Soviet Defense Minister was dismissed as a result of the flight.

Scientist destroying gene-altered trees

Sept 3. A plant researcher who violated federal rules by injecting genetically engineered bacteria into 14 young elms today ended his experiment by cutting down the trees. The scientist, Gary Strobel of Montana State University, neglected to get federal approval before injecting the trees with bacteria designed to fight Dutch elm disease. He ran afoul of federal rules intended to avoid environmental damage from genetic engineering experiments. Strobel said he cut down the trees to avoid federal penalties against other university research.

Central America faces severe social crisis

A characteristically large family crowds into a small room in a village in Central America, a region in the midst of its worst crisis in this century.

Beneath the surface of the violent political conflicts that dominate the news about Central America is a severe social crisis rooted in overpopulation, land hunger and poverty, according to a report in this week's New York Times.

Spiraling population growth is a primary cause of the region's turmoil. The population of Costa Rica, El Salvador, Guatemala, Honduras and Nicaragua exceeds 25 million, double the figure of 25 years ago.

"The population growth rate is one of the highest in the world," said one expert. "Demographic factors are tremendously important; they will continue to play a major role not only in our social, economic and political situation, but also in the generation of violence."

The population crisis feeds a hunger for land. Millions of peasants have no hope of living decent lives because they have no way to grow food. And most land reform efforts have either failed or proved to be disappointing. "There is land, plenty of land, where I come from," said a Guatemalan peasant. "But there is none for a poor man like me."

A steady job is a dream for over half the population, leading to mass poverty among workers. "The government has done nothing for the majority of us," said a Salvadoran electrician. "Life is worse for the workers." All of these conditions make for fertile ground for the growth of Marxist guerrilla groups.

SEPTEMBER
Week 37 1987

Su	Mo	Tu	We	Th	Fr	Sa
		1	2	3	4	5
6	7	8	9	10	11	12
13	14	15	16	17	18	19
20	21	22	23	24	25	26
27	28	29	30			

6. Rome: U.S. finishes third in total medals at world track and field championships.

6. Newark, N.J.: National Assn. for Aid to Fat Americans holds national convention.

6. Baltimore: Siamese twins, joined at head, separated in 22-hour operation.→

7. Pittsburgh: Jesse Jackson officially declares candidacy in presidential race (→ 13).

7. U.S.: Study reports high schools foster elitism with inadequate education in humanities for the non-college bound.

8. N.Y.: Govt. report claims much of city's construction industry accepts Mafia as force for stability and profitability.

8. Dearborn, Mich.: U.A.W. proposes job guarantee in new Ford pact, reflecting labor's shift from wages to job security.

9. Washington: In second-largest federal rescue of ailing bank, FDIC saves First City Bancorporation of Texas with $1 bil.

9. Manila: Cabinet quits in effort to force resignation of Aquino aide Joker Arroyo (→ 17).

10. Washington: Census Bureau says U.S. Hispanic population grows at five times average rate.

10. Washington: Reagan administration presents plea for $270 million in contra aid (→ 20).

10. N.Y.: Western industrial nations, at U.N., defeat Soviet plan to give funds saved through arms pacts to Third World debt.

11. Washington: U.S. trade deficit hits record $16.5 billion for July (→ 16).

11. Toronto: Liberals win Ontario election in setback to ruling Conservative Party.

11. N.Y.: Original Winnie-the-Pooh, now 65 years old, goes on display in N.Y. Public Library.

12. New York: Martina Navratilova beats Steffi Graf 7-6, 6-1 in final of U.S. Open.

DEATHS

11. Lorne Greene, star of TV's "Bonanza" (*2/12/1915).

11. Peter Tosh, founder of The Wailers, Reggae band.

Pope in U.S. against background of dissent

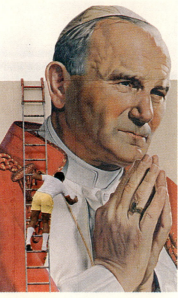

A billboard in Miami of Pope John Paul II gets a last-minute makeover.

Sept 12. As Pope John Paul II makes a historic tour of the South and Southwest, he is continuously faced with disagreement about several key Church doctrines. The critics, however, are not members of a competing religion, or even atheists; they are Roman Catholics, both laity and priests, who are turning out in droves for the pope's appearances.

A recent series of New York Times/CBS News polls has found that, in a random sample of American Roman Catholics, many question papal infallibility on such subjects as birth control, abortion, divorce, homosexuality, ordination of women as priests and the requisite vow of celibacy for Catholic priests.

Fifty-eight percent of all Catholics questioned believed the Church should change some of its teachings to reflect the opinions of most Catholics. Fifty-five percent of priests surveyed believed that they should have the right to marry. Dissent among American Catholics was a "serious problem," the pope said when he appeared in Miami on September 10, but there is "a great silent majority which is faithful" (→ 15).

Siamese twins, joined at heads, separated

Sept 6. Two seven-month-old Siamese twin boys who were joined at the head were separated successfully by surgeons at Johns Hopkins Hospital in Baltimore in a 22-hour operation that ended this morning. The twins, Patrick and Benjamin Binder, were flown here from West Germany for the operation, during which their hearts were stopped and their bodies chilled to permit the delicate surgery. Doctors say it will take weeks to determine whether the operation succeeded. No previous effort to separate such twins has been totally successful.

East German Communist chief visits Bonn

Honecker is greeted with anger.

Sept 8. As he wound up his historic trip to Bonn, the first by an East German Communist Party chief, Erich Honecker reaffirmed the differences that separate the two countries, even as he pledged to maintain contacts. "Fireside dreams are far from our minds," he said. "We take the existence of two sovereign states on German soil for granted." In meetings with West German Chancellor Helmut Kohl, Honecker agreed to more scientific cooperation and environmental protection. But he would not cancel the order to shoot anyone trying to cross the Berlin Wall. Honecker, 75, was born in Wiebelskirchen, now a part of West Germany.

Summer movies set record of $1.6 bil.

Sept 8. The heat is gone, but the profits linger. Summer movies brought in a little under $1.6 billion dollars, a record surpassing 1984 (the year of "Ghostbusters," "The Karate Kid" and "Indiana Jones and the Temple of Doom"). There were fewer big hits this summer -- just a lot of little ones. Higher ticket prices and a late Labor Day helped hike the sum, too. "La Bamba," about 50's rock singer Richie Valens, had an infectiously pleasing sound track. "The Untouchables," "The Witches of Eastwick" and "Predator" were other teen-pleasers, but the topper at $150 million was "Beverly Hills Cop II" with Eddie Murphy.

Angola battles on; fight ten years old

Sept 9. More than ten years after gaining independence from Portugal, Angola is still fighting a civil war. Jonas Savimbi's National Union for the Total Independence of Angola (known by its Portuguese acronym, UNITA), enjoys the support of the United States, South Africa and other friendly African countries. UNITA forces continue to thwart the better-equipped Soviet-backed and Cuban-reinforced Angolan army. And Savimbi still hopes to force Angola's Marxist government, led by President Jose Eduardo dos Sontos, into a coalition.

UNITA chief Savimbi and rebels.

50,000 forest fires leave heavy damage

A forest fire, a striking sight at night, is nonetheless deadly to people.

The annual ring of fire is hitting extra hard this year. Every hour, dozens of forest fires erupt in the nation's dry areas, bringing the total so far close to 50,000.

Trees ablaze, terrified people fleeing with pets and hastily collected belongings, struggling firefighters, millions of dollars in timber up in smoke, and destroyed homes are part of the picture.

Yet, what to us spells tragedy is nature's way of ending and beginning natural cycles. The Indians knew this and ignited fires to open up hunting grounds, stimulate growth and wipe out infestations.

Today, however, we have populated and invested in these areas and must heed Smokey the Bear's admonitions. With care, we could prevent half of the conflagrations. The other half are started by nature itself—by lightning.

Rather walks off, leaving CBS dark

Sept 11. Many viewers of the CBS Evening News saw six minutes of black Friday when anchorman Dan Rather angrily walked off the set after being told that U.S. Open tennis coverage would delay his broadcast. Rather left the set shortly after 6:30 p.m., but when the match ended at 6:33, control of the time went to CBS News and the screen went blank. He was rushed back and anchored the broadcast.

Reagan rebuked by Thurgood Marshall

Sept 8. Justice Thurgood Marshall, the only black ever to sit on the United States Supreme Court, said in a television interview that he ranked Ronald Reagan at "the bottom" of U.S. Presidents in terms of civil rights. Marshall placed Presidents Truman and Johnson at the top of his list. It is extremely rare for a Supreme Court justice to criticize a president in comments off the bench (→ 17).

Biden appropriates British leader's words

Sept 11. "Why is it that Joe Biden is the first in his family ever to go to a university? ..." Spontaneous? Well, not exactly, even though Senator Joseph R. Biden Jr. claimed that the thought had just come to him on his way to a debate at the Iowa State Fair last month in his quest for the presidential nomination on the Democratic ticket.

It now turns out that the senator's speech closely resembled one given by Neil Kinnock, the Labor Party leader who sought but lost the post of Prime Minister in Britain. Aides to the senator say that he was not trying to "put something over" on his audience. Said one top Biden aide: "He was on automatic pilot" (→ 17).

Work of two noted photographers shown

Sept 12. Exhibitions of the work of two of the century's greatest photographers opened this week in New York. Ninety early pictures by Henri Cartier-Bresson, most of them made between 1932 and 1934, are on view at The Museum of Modern Art, while The Metropolitan Museum of Art is featuring 120 photographs that span Edward Weston's entire career.

Cartier-Bresson, after studying painting in the early twenties, experimented with photography in 1929, and in 1932 he acquired a hand-held Leica. The camera enabled him to follow the action as it unfolded. Inspired by Surrealism, which he described as "a revolt in art but also in life," the young Frenchman went on to capture on film in the next three years a unique realm of cheap hotels, poor neighborhoods and brothels. "I prowled the streets all day, feeling very strung-up, ready to pounce, determined to trap life," he later wrote. After World War II, he gained fame as a photojournalist.

Weston, born in Illinois, decided at age 16 that photography would be his career, after his father gave him a simple box camera. His pictorialist period (1914-22) of studio portraits was followed by an appreciation and mastery of pure form, as seen in his famous photos of seashells, vegetables and nudes.

Cartier-Bresson's "Trieste" (1933), stark and haunting in black and white, reflects the artist's belief that color lessens the expressiveness of a photo.

"Nude" (1936), by Edward Weston, shows the photographer's fascination with sculptural form during the 1930's. Weston was influenced by Alfred Stieglitz.

Su	Mo	Tu	We	Th	Fr	Sa
		1	2	3	4	5
6	7	8	9	10	11	12
13	14	15	16	17	18	19
20	21	22	23	24	25	26
27	28	29	30			

13. Iowa: Pat Robertson tops GOP contenders for presidency in statewide straw poll (→ 17).

13. Sri Lanka: Tamil separatists kill 68 in rival militant group (→ 10/7).

14. Washington: Elizabeth Dole quits as transportation secretary to aid husband's campaign.

14. New York: Ivan Lendl beats Mats Wilander 6-7, 6-0, 7-6, 6-4 for third straight U.S. Open win.

14. Washington: Reagan meets with Roh Tae Woo, South Korean ruling party candidate (→ 10/9).

14. Washington: Population Crisis Committee reports U.K. leads developed world in providing birth control services.

14. U.S.: Reynolds Corp. announces new "smokeless" cigarette, to be marketed in 1988.

15. Bonn: West German computer enthusiasts said to have accessed international NASA network for three months.

15. Hollywood: Pope urges media leaders to shun violence, sex and fantasy (→ 19).

16. N.Y.: Dow dives 36.39, putting two-day loss at 82.25 (→ 22).

16. Washington: Pentagon report charges sexual harassment in Navy and Marine Corps.

16. London: Midland Bank accepts $160 million in raw materials as partial payment of Peruvian debt in first such pact.

17. Washington: Alan Keyes, highest ranking black in State Dept., quits, charging racism.

17. Washington: Preliminary congressional report says money for contras was driving force behind Iran arms sale (→ 26).

17. Manila: Aquino, bowing to political pressure, fires Joker Arroyo, her closest adviser (→ 10/28).

18. Washington: Reagan announces mid- and short-range missile pact will be signed at summit later this year (→ 10/23).

DEATH

13. Mervyn LeRoy, film director, "Little Caesar," "Quo Vadis" (*10/15/1900).

We the People celebrate Constitution

Howard Chandler Christy's "Scene at the Signing of the Constitution of the United States."

Sept 17. With some help from Hollywood and a production team from Radio City Music Hall, bells rang, the President waved and flags were unfurled in Philadelphia today to celebrate the 200th birthday of the Constitution. Balloons festooned Constitution Hall as Warren Burger, who quit his job as Chief Justice to organize the bicentennial celebrations, struck a reproduction of the Liberty Bell.

A statue of George Washington towered over President Reagan as he spoke of the significance of the occasion. "In a very real sense, it was then, in 1787, that the revolution began," the president said. He also acknowledged that the atmosphere was far from festive 200 years ago. "In fact," Reagan said, "the Constitution and our government were born in crisis. The years leading up to the constitutional convention were some of the most difficult our nation has endured."

Some political observers speculated that the problems facing the Reagan administration focused even greater attention on the bicentennial observances. "A whole batch of things have caused Americans to be more interested in the Constitution," Cornell historian Michael Kammen told The New York Times. The tug of war between the Congress and the White House over the Iran-contra affair is highlighting the use and possible abuse of presidential power. In addition, the controversial nomination of Robert Bork to the Supreme Court raises questions about how strictly the Constitution should be interpreted. Reagan made an indirect reference to the nomination by saying the judiciary should exercise "restraint."

Weighty constitutional matters, however, were far from the minds of most of the people who descended on Philadelphia and congregated on the banks of the Delaware for the "Great American Picnic." Constitutional issues were also seldom discussed by Brent Musberger, the network sports commentator who anchored coverage of the events.

The festivities were enlivened by the Mormon Tabernacle Choir, which sang the national anthem. College bands from all over the country performed a new composition by Peter Nero. Thirty floats participated in a two-mile parade produced by Radio City Music Hall Productions.

Unless they run out of steam, the bicentennial observances will continue for another four years. The actual establishment of the federal government still has to be celebrated. So do the beginnings of the Congress, the presidency and the courts. Not to mention the 200th birthday of the Bill of Rights in 1991.

An eagle and pen grace the face of the Constitution Gold Coin.

Bork hearing leaves his future in doubt

Sept 19. Judge Robert H. Bork, a hero of the right, ended five grueling days of testimony today, insisting that his philosophy is "neither liberal nor conservative." But many members, perhaps even a majority, of the Senate Judiciary Committee considering his fitness to be a Supreme Court justice, were not convinced.

Seeking to repackage himself as a moderate, the 60-year-old former Yale law professor, who flirted with socialism as a youth, appeared to have failed to erase concern over past positions on such issues as sex discrimination, free speech and privacy, despite his insistence that he has "no ideological agenda" and has "great respect for precedent."

He vowed repeatedly that once on the high court he would be guided not by "some personal political agenda of my own" or by a "desire to set the social agenda" of the nation, but by the Constitution. "I am a jurist who believes his role is to interpret the law and not make it," he said (→ 10/6).

Pope bans dissent

Sept 19. When urged by United States Roman Catholic Bishops to honor the freedom of speech which Americans prize so highly, the Pope replied that dissent was incompatible with being Catholic. Ending his visit to the United States in Detroit, John Paul also spoke vehemently against abortion.

Biden says he made law school mistake

Sept 17. Fighting to salvage his presidential campaign, Senator Joseph R. Biden Jr. acknowleged today he had made "a mistake" in his youth, when he plagiarized a law review article for a paper he wrote in his first year in law school. But the Delaware Democrat, while conceding he had done some "dumb things," said that the recent disclosures that he had used material from others' political speeches without attribution was "much ado about nothing" (→ 23).

Nations in accord to save ozone layer

Sept 16. Alarmed by scientific reports that the earth's ozone shield is shrinking, delegates from more than 70 nations approved an agreement to limit use of the chemicals believed to be doing the damage.

Under the agreement, use of the chemicals will first be frozen at existing levels and then will be reduced by 50 percent by 1999. The action, taken at the end of a meeting in Montreal, resulted from convincing evidence that ozone at the upper edge of the atmosphere is being destroyed by chlorofluorocarbons, which are used in air conditioners, refrigerators, aerosol sprays and other products. Destruction of the ozone layer allows more dangerous ultraviolet radiation to reach the earth's surface and also has unpredictable effects on climate.

The United States limited use of chlorofluorocarbons in the 1970's, but most other nations did not. The observations that spurred them to act include reports of a "hole" in the ozone layer that appears over the South Pole each year.

Internees repaid

Sept 17. The House has passed a bill which will provide an apology and about $20,000 to each of 66,000 Japanese-American survivors of United States detainment camps. Over 120,000 Japanese-American civilians were held under armed guard for three and a half years during World War II.

New boy on block buys more papers

Sept 14. Less than four years ago, William Dean Singleton had neither newspapers nor wealth. Using his own drive and other people's funds, he has built an empire. The 36-year-old Texan runs a newspaper chain of 28 dailies and 28 weeklies from Connecticut to California. Now his Media News Group Inc. is buying The Denver Post and The Houston Post for $95 and $110 million respectively. The chain's worth is estimated to be $1.2 billion, and Singleton owns roughly a third.

Michael Jackson opens world tour in Tokyo

Michael Jackson, on tour to promote his long-awaited new album, "Bad."

Sept 13. He's been labeled an eccentric recluse by much of the world's press, and his new album got mixed reviews, but tonight Michael Jackson triumphed before 40,000 ecstatic Tokyo fans. Jackson arrived last week for the opening of a new world tour, and he and his constant companion, a pet chimp named Bubbles, have created a media sensation. Tonight, Tokyo fans saw an extravagant show featuring lasers and dazzling choreography. They had no trouble accepting Jackson's new image, dramatically altered by cosmetic facial surgery, and lovingly chanted his Japanese name, "Mykeru," between songs from "Bad," his new album, and "Thriller," his 1983 mega-hit.

"60 Minutes" enters 20th season on CBS

Sept 16. The TV networks love a ratings hit, and CBS has the big one. "60 Minutes," the Sunday night news magazine, jumps into its 20th season this week, and it shows no signs of slowing down. The show ranks consistently in the top 10, and it makes CBS a bundle of money. This year, as CBS struggles through a reevaluation and budget cuts, "60 Minutes" is still the jewel of the news division. Mike Wallace heads its roster of journalism superstars. Morley Safer, Harry Reasoner, Diane Sawyer, Ed Bradley and humorist Andy Rooney are the other contributors. Don Hewitt is the Executive Producer.

Harry Reasoner, Diane Sawyer, Morley Safer, Mike Wallace and Ed Bradley.

Su	Mo	Tu	We	Th	Fr	Sa
		1	2	3	4	5
6	7	8	9	10	11	12
13	14	15	16	17	18	19
20	21	22	23	24	25	26
27	28	29	30			

20. Managua: Nicaragua ends ban on opposition paper La Prensa (→ 22).

20. "Mandela" aired on HBO; Jerry Falwell and Citizens for Reagan urge boycott (→ 11/5).

21. Persian Gulf: U.S. attacks Iranian vessel caught laying mines; three killed (→ 10/8).

21. New York: Tiffany's celebrates 150th anniversary.

22. N.Y.: Dow, spurred by low deficit projection, surges 75.23 in largest one-day gain (→ 30).

22. N.Y.: Rep. Mario Biaggi and Meade Esposito convicted of accepting unlawful gratuities, acquitted on bribery charges.

22. Managua: Ban lifted on Roman Catholic radio station, closed for 21 months (→ 10/3).

22. Poland, U.S. agree to resume ties (→ 10/10).

24. Film "Fatal Attraction" grosses $10 mil. in first week.

24. Baltimore: Moscow Ballet makes U.S. debut.

25. Suva, Fiji: Col. Rabuka stages coup three days before bipartisan govt. was to be installed.

27. Washington, N.J.: Dalai Lama, at end of 12-day U.S. visit, denounces Chinese moves to dominate Tibet (→ 10/9).

28. Denver: Rep. Pat Schroeder declares she will not enter presidential race (→ 30).

28. Tehran: Mehdi Hashemi, Iranian aide linked to U.S. arms deal, executed by firing squad.

28. U.S.: Avis sold to employees for $1.75 billion.

28. N.Y.: Jury awards $78 million to model Marla Hanson, victim of slashing attack.

29. Washington: Congress halts aid to Pakistan, pending talks on nuclear capabilities.

29. U.S.: "The Old Farmer's Almanac" goes on sale with first color cover in 196 years.

DEATHS

22. Dan Rowan, ex-host of TV's "Laugh-In" (*7/22/1922).

25. Mary Astor, actress, born Lucile Langhanke, starred in "Maltese Falcon" (*5/3/1906).

Senator Biden gives up presidential bid

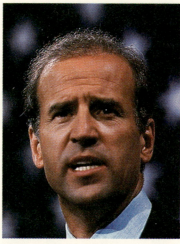

Biden: Pathological plagiarizer?

Sept 23. Senator Joseph R. Biden Jr. withdrew from the race for president today, saying that his bid for the Democratic nomination had been dashed by "the exaggerated shadow" of his own mistakes. He is the second of this year's field of Democratic candidates to drop out.

Unlike former Senator Gary Hart, whose withdrawal speech centered on invective against the media, Senator Biden betrayed little bitterness but some sadness as he made known his decision. "I made some mistakes," he said.

In recent weeks, the senator has admitted he plagiarized a law review article while in law school. He also has been accused of using the words of others in campaign speeches, without attribution. Senator Biden told a crowded news conference that he had to choose between trying to save his campaign or fulfilling his role as chairman of the Senate Judiciary Committee, which is conducting hearings on Judge Robert Bork's Supreme Court nomination (→ 28).

Mattingly hits 6th grand slam of year

Sept 30. Don Mattingly of the Yankees continued his season of record-busting by walloping his sixth grand slam homer of the year. He smashed a pitch off Bruce Hurst of the Red Sox into right field for a 6-0 victory. "It feels good to do this, something nobody has ever done," he said. Until this season, he had never hit a grand slam in the majors. The 12-year-old boy who caught the ball got a Yankee hat, a team picture, two gloves and Don's bat. Don got the ball.

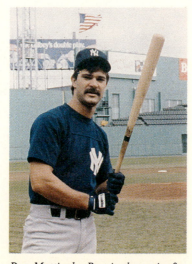

Don Mattingly: Best in the majors?

50 millionth VCR shipped to market

Sept 27. Twelve years ago, Sony introduced the first video cassette recorder. Today, the 50 millionth VCR was shipped to market, and now over half the homes in America are equipped with the machines. Sales are expected to top 13.5 million by the end of 1987, leading one spokesman to say "this will be our best year in history."

While Americans love to rent a tape and spend a couple of hours with Bogart or Hepburn, they also have a passion for recording their own proms, weddings and birthdays. Sales of camcorders (combination VCR-cameras) jumped 39 percent in the past year. Experts predict that other innovations, such as sharper picture resolution, in the new VCR will spread the gadget to two-thirds of American homes.

Economy enters 3rd longest growth period

Sept 30. The United States entered its 59th consecutive month of economic growth, according to the Commerce Department, the third longest period of expansion on record, and the longest in peacetime.

The news provides Republicans ammunition for the 1988 elections. In a speech yesterday, President Reagan said he had helped start a worldwide "revolution in economic thinking," based on the idea that "the best thing government can do is get out of the way."

But critics noted recent U.S. growth was spurred substantially by burgeoning foreign investment. They predicted increasing U.S. resources will be used to pay dividends and interest to foreigners in years to come.

Aside from foreign investment, experts noted other factors in the U.S. growth: high consumer demand, the increased productivity of maturing baby-boomers in the labor force, low inflation rates and Reagan's military buildup (→ 10/6).

Cuppa declining as fashion in Britain

A hallowed tradition is crumbling in England. Tea has been a lubricant of thought and speech in the country since the 19th century, when Anna, seventh Duchess of Bedford, declared the tea ritual the best antidote to late afternoon blues. However, to young Britons today, it seems that tea drinking has acquired an old-fashioned, dowdy image, and in the last decade the volume of tea consumed has fallen more than 20 percent. They still drink two cups of tea for every one cup of the more expensive coffee, but in 1966 the ratio was six to one.

Tammy's "Ballad of Jim and Tammy" is a big hit in the South.

Bill Cosby, the man and his millions

The success of Bill Cosby can lead one to ask the age-old question, "Can you ever have too much of a good thing?" Cosby is omnipresent: in his top-rated TV show; on bookshelves (his volume "Time Flies" just swept into stores); in commercials (he is a pitchman for Kodak, E.F. Hutton and Jell-O); and doing stand-ups on stage in Las Vegas and New York—seemingly simultaneously.

What drives Cosby? He doesn't need the money, Time magazine reports. The highest-paid entertainer in America, he will earn about $57 million this year. It sccms instead that idleness was never penned into Cosby's cosmic schedule. Even earlier in his career, making shows like "I Spy," Cosby kept busy—getting a degree in

Bill Cosby, media miracle.

education at the University of Massachusetts and as a guest on Sesame Street. He turned 50 in July—and will probably celebrate it soon if he can just pencil it in.

Henry Ford II, auto heir, dies at 70

Sept 29. Henry Ford II, who rescued the second largest auto firm in the United States from bankruptcy, died of pneumonia in Detroit today. A noted philanthropist, the automotive tycoon established the Ford Foundation and helped rebuild downtown Detroit. Ford led a tempestuous personal and professional life. He was married three times and was known in the industry as a tyrannical boss who fired anyone who threatened his power, including Lee Iacocca, now Chairman of Chrysler.

Dukakis aides quit in Biden scandal

Sept 30. Two top aides to Governor Michael S. Dukakis resigned from his presidential campaign staff today after the governor admitted that one of them had given reporters a videotape that helped destroy the candidacy of a Democratic rival, Senator Joseph R. Biden Jr. The tape had juxtaposed a speech by Biden with one by Neil Kinnock, the British Labor Party leader. In a speech last spring, Senator Biden had used Kinnock's almost exact words without any attribution (→ 10/1).

Stage and screen mourn Bob Fosse

Fosse, driven at high speed.

Sept 24. Famed director and choreographer Bob Fosse, collapsed on the street and died of a heart attack Wednesday night before the opening of his show "Sweet Charity" in Washington. He was 60. Fosse's work was widely acclaimed in Hollywood and on Broadway. In 1973, he became the only director ever to win a Tony ("Pippin"), an Oscar ("Cabaret") and an Emmy ("Liza With a Z") in the same year. Actor Joel Grey said what he would remember about Fosse is "the dance vocabulary he invented." In 1979, after open-heart surgery, Fosse made "All That Jazz," a film about a chain-smoking director-choreographer who dies of a heart attack.

NFL players strike on free agent issue

Sept 22. The chances for a normal season were thrown for a loss today when the National Football League Players Association voted to strike. The association, which represents 1,500 players with an average salary of $230,000, decided to walk out unless their demands—chiefly one protecting free agency—are met. "As of midnight tonight, the players of the NFL are on strike," said Gene Upshaw on television at halftime of the Jets-Patriots game. Free agency protects the right of a player to change teams after a contract with one team has expired. The league owners have said they will try to salvage the season by enlisting players previously cut from the squad (→ 10/16).

Ms. Magazine sold to Australian firm

Sept 23. Ms. Magazine, which has served as an influential forum for the women's movement for 15 years, will be sold fo Fairfax Publications, one of Australia's largest publishers. Yesterday's announcement ended a search by Gloria Steinem and Patricia Carbine, co-founders, for new money to expand. They will remain as consultants for five years and Anne Summers, an Australian journalist, will become Editor-in-Chief. The company is committed to maintaining the magazine's feminist policies.

Woodward-Casey, a deathbed scene

BOB WOODWARD

VEIL:
The Secret
Wars of the
CIA 1981-1987

Woodward's big scoop this year.

Sept 26. "Veil: The Secret Wars of the CIA," a new book by Washington Post editor Bob Woodward, charges former CIA Director William Casey, who died in May, went outside agency channels and personally arranged for Saudi Arabia to sponsor a car bomb attack against a Lebanese Shiite leader suspected of terrorism against Americans. The bombing killed 62 people, but not its target, Sheik Mohammed Hussein Fadlallah, of the so-called Party of God. In the book, Woodward also claims that he met briefly with Casey as he lay dying in a hospital room, and that when asked if he had directed the Iran-contra operation, Casey nodded that he had (→ 10/4).

The latest toy for the young, upwardly mobile professional is the Jeep, 47 years after its debut. Says one salesman: "They're trading in BMWs."

Su	Mo	Tu	We	Th	Fr	Sa
				1	2	3
4	5	6	7	8	9	10
11	12	13	14	15	16	17
18	19	20	21	22	23	24
25	26	27	28	29	30	31

1. Brooklyn: Pat Robertson enters race for Republican presidential nomination (→ 8).

1. Johnny Carson marks 25th anniversary of "Tonight Show."

1. Johannesburg: Pat Anthony gives birth to daughter's triplets in unique surrogate mother case.

2. Washington: Michael Deaver, in perjury case, claims alcoholism impaired memory.

2. Finland: AIDS found to elude detection for up to year in some cases (→ 13).

3. Washington: Reagan administration lists demands for Sandinistas, overstepping requirements of Arias peace accord (→ 8).

4. U.S.: Government Accounting Office says State Dept. ran illegal propaganda operation to gain aid for contras (→ 11/16).

4. Mexico: Institutional Revolutionary Party names Carlos Salinas de Gortari for president.

4. San Salvador: President Duarte meets with rebel leaders first time in three years (→ 26).

5. Springsteen's "Tunnel of Love" album hits record stores.

6. Washington: Senate panel disapproves of Bork nomination (→ 23).

6. New York: Dow drops record 91.55 on fears over rising interest rates and dollar (→ 12).

6. N.Y.: Yale Club, where men swam nude, admits women, as long as they wear bathing suits.

7. Dominican Republic: 50 killed by drowning and sharks as launch sinks on way to U.S.

7. Sri Lanka: Tamil rebels kill over 160, provoking India to send troops (→ 12).

8. Persian Gulf: U.S. helicopters sink three Iranian boats; Iran denounces act of war (→ 16):

9. Seoul: Kim Young Sam declares candidacy, widening split in Korean opposition (→ 12).

10. Warsaw: Premier Zbigniew Messner announces plan for wide reform, mixing capitalism and socialism (→ 11/14).

DEATH

9. Clare Boothe Luce, playwright, editor, diplomat and politician (* 4/10/1903).

California 'quake kills six, injures 100

Oct 1. A violent earthquake measuring 6.1 on the Richter scale slammed the Los Angeles area this morning. Six people are reported dead; some were killed by falling debris while others succumbed to heart failure. About 100 people are in area hospitals with injuries.

The earthquake had its epicenter at Whittier, a town 20 miles east of Los Angeles. At 7:42 a.m., people getting ready to leave for work dropped their coffee cups, grabbed their children and raced out of doors. Some did not escape their buckling buildings in time; one, a student at California State University of Los Angeles, was crushed by a concrete slab that fell off a school parking facility.

When the tremors faded, Los Angeles residents were in a sense relieved. This was not the "big" one. That earthquake, predicted for many years, will develop along the San Andreas Fault line (this quake

Cars lie crushed by bricks from a collapsing building in Los Angeles.

came from the weaker Whittier Fault) and strike the area with an intensity 60 times greater. On the other hand, this quake did nothing to forestall the future.

Relentlessly mellow, Southern Californians resumed their leisure activities. By noon, Disneyland at Anaheim was back in action, with crowds in line for the roller coaster.

Victory in Nicaragua: Prensa reappears

Oct 8. "The People Triumph; La Prensa Uncensored." With that banner headline, Nicaragua's opposition newspaper, La Prensa, has hit the newsstands for the first time in 451 days. The printing of the paper shows a willingness by the Sandinista regime to abide by this summer's Central American peace plan. Nicaraguan President Daniel Ortega acted to open La Prensa

earlier than the accord requires, which is November 7.

President Ortega also declared a unilateral cease-fire in three areas of conflict in the Sandinista-contra war. In a speech at the United Nations, Ortega assailed the Reagan administration's call for continued arms support to the contras. That prompted a walk-out by the American delegation (→ 14).

Abused girl jailed for father's murder

Oct 5. Two murder cases implicating teenagers had different outcomes today: one teen was cleared and one was not. Cheryl Pierson, an 18-year-old girl from Selden, L.I., was sentenced to six months in jail for plotting her father's murder. Miss Pierson, who said her father sexually abused her for several years, hired a classmate two years ago to gun him down in front of her home. That friend, Sean Pica, received a 24-year prison sentence.

In Elkland, Mo., 14-year-old Kirk Buckner was charged last week with shooting his brothers, parents and an aunt. The chief witness was his uncle, James Schnick, who claimed he was attacked like the others but survived. Neighbors were devastated—and confounded. Kirk had always been a good boy, they said. And how, they wondered, could the 90-pound youngster drag his father's body the great distance it was found from home?

Schnick was arraigned in court today, confessing he was the killer. Kirk can't celebrate. He died last week in what is no longer judged a suicide.

Publisher Chamorro: "The People Triumph; La Prensa Uncensored."

Canada, U.S. agree to cut trade barriers

Oct 4. The United States and Canada have agreed on a trade pact that would eliminate tariffs and other trade barriers between the two countries by the year 2000. The agreement came after 16 months of negotiations during which Canada broke off talks when the United States would not agree to bar future protectionist actions.

Under the agreement, all tariffs will be ended over a ten-year period beginning Jan. 1, 1989. The effect will be to give U.S. firms increased access to a market the size of California while allowing Canada to increase exports of wood products, metals and other natural resources, where it has an advantage.

The pact is regarded as a model for improved international trade at

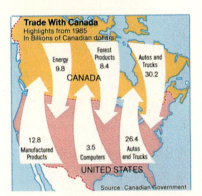

The United States and Canada are the world's largest trading partners.

a time when many nations are considering more barriers. Canadian Finance Minister Michael Wilson called it "a win-win situation" that benefits both countries.

Herald-Trib marks birthday in Paris

Oct 4. It was 100 years ago today that the first issue of The New York Herald hit the streets of Paris. This week, the newspaper—now the International Herald Tribune – celebrated. A "global newspaper," the U.S.-owned Trib is published in Singapore, London, Paris, Zurich, Rome, The Hague, Hong Kong, Marseilles and Miami. Publisher Lee W. Huebner calls it "a hometown newspaper for a lot of people who have a lot of hometowns." One out of ten readers is said to be a millionaire.

John Vinocur, Executive Editor of the International Herald Tribune.

Space monkey is in the driver's seat

Oct 7. A monkey aboard a Soviet research satellite has broken loose from its restraints and is causing such mischief that the mission might have to be ended, Tass said today. The monkey is named Yeroshka, Russian for troublemaker. It managed to free its left arm and is punching buttons at random, Tass said, endangering a mission designed to pave the way for manned interplanetary flights. Soviet controllers might bring the spacecraft back to earth for "humanitarian reasons," Tass said (→ 26).

Founder of child's newspaper is dead

Oct 9. Eleanor M. Johnson's 4-foot 10-inch frame belied the weighty accomplishments of her 94 years. She earned two master's degrees and created over 50 school workbooks. But after her death today, the former editor will be remembered for The Weekly Reader, read by two-thirds of Americans while they were in grade school. The first edition covered the 1928 presidential race. The headline on Al Smith and Herbert Hoover read, "Two Poor Boys Who Made Good Are Now Running for the Highest Office in the World."

Tibetans demand freedom; Chinese kill six

Oct 9. For the past 29 days, Lhasa, the capital and religious center of Tibet, has been the site of protests and riots by Tibetans, including many Buddhist monks and lamas, calling for independence from Chinese Communist rule.

China has controlled Tibet since the 1950's, when it staged an invasion and forced the Dalai Lama, the traditional political and spiritual leader of the mountainous region, into exile.

Clashes between protesters and Chinese police over the past week, in which at least six Tibetans, including three monks, were killed, marks the first violence directed against Chinese rule in more than ten years. Chinese officials blamed the Dalai Lama, who was visiting the United States at the time, for instigating the riot.

The Chinese have also expelled foreign journalists from the area, declaring that 14 news reporters from six countries were in Tibet illegally and that reporting on the anti-Chinese activity was prohibited.

A Tibetan Buddhist lies in front of a Lhasa police station burned by protesters.

U.A.W. blasts Bush praise for Russians

Oct 2. Vice President George Bush ran head-on into big trouble today when he lauded the ability of Soviet mechanics, saying that when they ran out of work in their own country, Moscow should "send them to Detroit." His comments were promptly criticized by Owen F. Beiber, President of the United Automobile Workers, as "foolish."

Bush, who is expected to seek the Republican nomination for the presidency, made his remarks in Brussels during his ten-day trip to Europe. Asked what he had learned during the trip, he marveled that the Soviet Union recently staged an operation involving 350 tanks without a single breakdown. Detroit, he observed, "could use that kind of ability."

Robertson admits lie about wedding

Oct 8. Pat Robertson, the former television evangelist now running for president, acknowledged today that he was married just ten weeks before his first child was born. "I have never, ever indicated that in the early part of my life I didn't sow some wild oats," the former Southern Baptist minister said. "I sowed plenty of them. But I also said that Jesus Christ came into my life, changed my life and forgave me."

Robertson, a conservative Republican popular with fundamentalist Christians, and his wife, Dede, were married August 27, 1954, in Elkton, Maryland, a favorite town for secret or quick marriages. Recently, Robertson said they were married in 1955 on March 22, which is his birthday (→ 12).

OCTOBER
Week 42 1987

Su	Mo	Tu	We	Th	Fr	Sa
				1	2	3
4	5	6	7	8	9	10
11	12	13	14	15	16	17
18	19	20	21	22	23	24
25	26	27	28	29	30	31

11. Hartford: Doug Jarvis, record-holder at 964 straight, misses first game of NHL career.

11. Scotland: Adrian Shine ends biggest search in Loch Ness after failure to find monster.

12. Sri Lanka: Indian paratroopers land in Jaffna Peninsula to fight Tamil guerrillas (→ 11/9).

12. Seoul: Assembly approves constitution providing for direct election of president (→ 27).

12. New York: Salomon Bros. to fire 12% of staff to cope with volatile Wall Street (→ 14).

13. Port-au-Prince: Haitian candidate Yves Volel assassinated; police suspected (→ 11/3).

14. New York: John Zaccaro, husband of ex-v.p. candidate, acquitted on bribery charges.

14. Argentine government announces drastic austerity plan.

14. U.S.: Trade gap down less than expected in August; Dow drops record 95.46 (→ 16).

14. New York: National Assn. of Sportswear names paisley Japanese tie "ugliest tie in America."

14. New Orleans: Ex-Transportation Secretary Elizabeth Dole has near-collision on plane.

15. Washington: New, unannounced Reagan policy will cut benefits for aged, blind and disabled (→ 16).

15. Dayton, Ohio: Two pit bull owners acquitted on charges of involuntary manslaughter.

16. Washington: Under heavy criticism, Reagan drops plan to cut benefits for poor.

16. Atlantic City: Mike Tyson stops Tyrell Biggs in seventh round after relentless battering.

16. Persian Gulf: U.S.-flagged tanker hit by Iranian missile in Kuwaiti waters (→ 19).

16. Ouagadougou: Capt. Thomas Sankara, deposed leader of Burkina Faso, executed along with 12 other officials.

16. U.S.: ABC presents last "Max Headroom" show, canceled for low ratings.

DEATH

12. Alf Landon, veteran Republican leader (*9/9/1887).

Gloved police arrest 600 in gay march

Oct. 13. Police donned gloves for protection today as they arrested about 600 persons during a demonstration by gay men and women seeking to enter the Supreme Court to protest a decision upholding the enforcement of a Georgia sodomy law against homosexuals. It was the largest mass arrest at the court since May Day of 1971, when 7,000 anti-war protesters were detained. "We have AIDS, we have rights," some of the protesters chanted as they sat on the court steps, jeering at the gloved policemen. The arrests and demonstration climaxed a week of protests in various parts of the nation by homosexuals and their political supporters (→ 27).

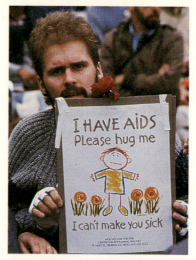
Fighting the stigma of AIDS.

Washington cops, gloved for protection, prepare to arrest demonstrators.

Sam Walton named richest American

Oct. 12. According to Forbes magazine's list of the 400 richest Americans, there are 49 billionaires in the country and the seat at the top is occupied by Sam Moore Walton, the 69-year-old founder of WalMart Stores, Inc. Walton, worth an incredible $8.5 billion, has been the number one man on Forbes' list for the last three years. The total number of billionaires in the United States is up from 26 last year. A billion one-dollar bills in a single stack would rise 123 miles, into outer space. Walton's astounding fortune would, stacked in singles, reach 1,045 miles into space.

Dow's weekly drop is largest since war

Oct. 16. The summer euphoria is over on Wall Street, and the market is tumbling dramatically. For the first time ever, the Dow Jones industrial average plunged more than 100 points today. It has dropped 235.48 points this week, the biggest weekly decline since World War II. "The salesmen couldn't really control their clients," one trader said. "They just wanted out." Investors are worried because of the huge trade deficit, the weak dollar and rising interest rates. Many of them are trading in their stocks for more stable Treasury bills and bonds. Since August, the Dow has declined almost 500 points (→ 19).

Nancy Reagan has operation for cancer

Oct. 17. Doctors said today that laboratory tests of tissue removed during Nancy Reagan's surgery for breast cancer showed no spread of the malignancy and that she has an excellent chance for full recovery. The First Lady's left breast was removed two days ago after doctors discovered a cancer about the width of a pencil, about as small as can be detected on a mammogram. This morning, Mrs. Reagan was up and about her suite at the Bethesda Naval Hospital. Later, she joined the President in telephoning the parents of Jessica McClure, a Texas child rescued from a well.

Arias wins Nobel for peace accord

Oct. 14. Costa Rican President Oscar Arias Sanchez, one day after winning the Nobel Peace Prize, has called on the Nicaraguan government to open talks with the contras. Yesterday's award, for Arias' role as author of the Central American peace plan, is sure to give added weight to the Guatemala accord.

The medicine prize went to Susumu Tonegawa, a Japanese scientist at M.I.T., for his work in immunology. Swiss scientists K. Alex Muller and J. Georg Bednorz took the prize in physics for discoveries in superconductivity. In chemistry, France's Jean-Marie Lehn and Americans Charles Pedersen and Donald Cram won for synthesizing organic compounds (→ 28).

Arias, architect of Latin peace plan.

NFL strike ends with no gain for players

NFL picket line in Philadelphia.

Oct 16. Representatives of the National Football League Players Association voted to return to work today, ending the 24-day-old strike. The union failed to achieve its major goal, unrestricted free agency, which would give players the right to move from one club to another after their contracts expire. Union chief Gene Upshaw said the association has filed a lawsuit against the NFL. He said the club owners "abused their monopoly powers to the extreme detriment of the players." Football fans can see their favorite players return to the field next week; the league told the union that striking players must wait a week before returning (→ 25).

Los Angeles trying year-round schools

Oct 13. Los Angeles schools, following the example of a handful of school districts nationwide, will begin a year-round school schedule beginning in July 1989. While the school year will still be 180 days long, vacation time will be split up into brief breaks two or three weeks in duration. Some educators feel students will retain information better and improve on tests with shorter breaks interrupting classes. The new schedule's main purpose, however, is to stagger usage of Los Angeles' overcrowded schools.

U.S., Soviet jointly study missile crisis

Oct 13. At an unusual three-day meeting at Harvard University, Soviet and American participants in the Cuban missile crisis of October 1962 agreed that Nikita Khrushchev's installation of missiles in Cuba was an adventurous move taken without deep consideration of the American reaction. The Soviet panelists said the missiles were installed because the Soviet Union was then convinced that a U.S. invasion of Cuba was imminent. But the American participants said no such invasion had been planned by the Kennedy administration. The Cuban missile crisis brought the world very close to nuclear war.

Business students lose $100,000 pay

Oct 13. Asher B. Edelman's normal domain is Wall Street. This year, he entered the halls of academia and brought the profit motive with him. The corporate takeover ace teaches "Corporate Raiding: The Art of War" at Columbia. As a final exam, he offered $100,000 to the student who could name a company for him to buy. Today, Dean John C. Burton halted the plan, saying it "would bias the academic environment." Says Edelman: "I'm trying to teach the students how to go out ... and take success."

Premier is named in Greek sex scandal

Oct 15. Affairs of the heart rarely intrude on affairs of state in Greece, but Athens is abuzz these days about a beautiful woman named Dimitra Liani. The 33-year-old former flight attendant has a new job as a television interviewer, thanks to the intervention of Prime Minister Andreas Papandreou. Some newspapers report that Papandreou's affair with Liani could be the last straw for his already shaky government. A conservative editor was incensed that Papandreou left his wife for a cruise with Liani and then failed to show up at ceremonies for victims of an earthquake in the small town of Kalamata.

Child rescued from Texas well shaft

Oct 16. "Humpty Dumpty had a great fall ..." The words echoed up to the ears of rescue workers, but the irony was lost on them. For 57 and a half hours, 18-month-old Jessica McClure was stuck in an abandoned well shaft, where she kept herself distracted if not amused by singing nursery rhymes. Volunteers operating drill equipment freed the little girl at 8 o'clock tonight. People worldwide prayed for the tot, and inhabitants of her tiny town of Midland, Texas, kept an around-the-clock vigil. Her teenage parents rejoice at her freedom.

It's official: Bush is now in the race

Oct 12. Vice President George Bush began his second quest for the presidency today, pledging to seek both harmony and tolerance. His formal announcement was made in Houston as he began a seven-day, cross-country swing. If elected, he would be the first sitting vice president since Martin Van Buren in 1836 to be elected president. Unlike 1980, when he lost the Republican nomination to Ronald Reagan, the vice president starts his presidential campaign this year well ahead of other contenders. He has already amassed $12.3 million in campaign funds (→ 11/9).

Raphael exhibit shows ninety drawings

Raphael, a master of the High Renaissance, lived for only 37 years (1483-1520). Apprenticed in his adolescence to the painter Perugino, he went on to work for popes, dukes and wealthy private patrons. His works adorn the Vatican Palace in Rome, Florence's Uffizi Palace and the Louvre in Paris.

A dazzling array of his drawings now graces the walls of New York's Pierpont Morgan Library. "Raphael and His Circle," includes some of the master's followers. Yet Raphael, to an attentive eye, stands head and shoulders above his disciples. Adding compassion to technical brilliance, he proves himself a genius at highlighting idiosyncracy without sacrificing universal form.

Raphael's "Head of a Young Man with Curly Hair; a Left Hand."

Su	Mo	Tu	We	Th	Fr	Sa
				1	2	3
4	5	6	7	8	9	10
11	12	13	14	15	16	17
18	19	20	21	22	23	24
25	26	27	28	29	30	31

18. Los Angeles: Baby born without brain kept alive to donate heart for transplant, a medical first.

19. Washington: John Stennis, 86, steps down after 40 years in Congress, second longest term.

19. St. Louis: Billy Martin named manager of N.Y. Yankees for fifth time.

19. Jakarta: 102 commuters killed as trains collide head-on.

19. Stockholm: Justice Minister Sten Wickbom resigns over escape of notorious spy Stig Bergling.

19. N.Y.: Stocks plunge 508 points; 22.6% drop nearly doubles 12.82% fall of 1929 (→ 20).

19. Rome: Measurements prove Everest to be 840 feet higher than K-2, resolving dispute.

21. N.Y.: Dow up record 186 points, recovering half of Monday's loss in two days (→ 22).

21. Stockholm: Nobel Prize in economics given to M.I.T. professor Robert M. Solow (→ 22).

22. U.S.: Dow falls 72.42; Reagan pledges budget talks with Congress (→ 26).

22. Stockholm: Exiled Soviet poet Joseph Brodsky wins Nobel Prize in literature.

22. New York: Joel Grey returns to Broadway in "Cabaret" for first time in two decades.

22. Washington: U.S. cuts exports to China over reported arms sales to Iran (→ 11/3).

22. Belleville, Ill.: Monsanto Co. fined $16.2 million for 1979 dioxin spill, ending one of longest jury trials in U.S. history.

23. Moscow: Gorbachev tells Shultz he will not meet with Reagan until S.D.I. is placed on bargaining table (→ 30).

23. Ethiopia: Rebels attack food convoy, halting drought aid.

24. Miami Beach: AFL-CIO votes Teamsters back into union after 30-year absence.

DEATHS

18. Dr. Philip Levine, found Rh factor in blood (*8/10/1900).

19. Jacqueline du Pre, British cellist (*1/26/1945).

U.S. hits Iran in reprisal

An Iranian oil platform burns in the Persian Gulf after the U.S. attack.

Oct 19. Retaliating for Iranian attacks on ships in the Persian Gulf, United States naval forces today damaged three offshore platforms said to be bases for Iran's gunboats.

Four American destroyers bombarded two of the platforms this afternoon, after giving Iranian crew members a 20-minute warning of the attack. A few hours later, commandos boarded a third platform and destroyed radar and communications equipment. The American attack came after heavy damage was done to an American-registered Kuwaiti tanker, the Sea Isle City, by a Chinese-made Silkworm missile fired from an Iranian base.

A statement by President Reagan described the action as a "prudent yet restrained response" to Iran's attacks on shipping. Defense Secretary Caspar Weinberger warned that "stronger countermeasures" might be taken if Iran did not stop its attacks. Congressional reaction was generally positive, but some members of Congress criticized the administration for not invoking the War Powers Resolution, which requires congressional approval of military actions. They said they feared American involvement in a Mideast conflict (→ 26).

Goetz is sentenced in subway shooting

Oct 19. Although acquitted of charges of assault and attempted murder stemming from the shooting on December 22, 1984, of four youths, Bernhard Goetz has been sentenced to six months in prison, a $5,000 fine and 280 hours of unpaid community service for possession of an unlicensed and concealed pistol. He also faces five years probation and will be required to undergo psychiatric couseling. Goetz has argued that he shot the youths, who are black, because they were threatening to mug him and that, although the city denied him a handgun license, he had a right to protect himself on the city's subways.

New tycoon Trump buys $30m yacht

Oct 19. Everyone loves a bargain, so when real estate tycoon Donald Trump discovered that the Sultan of Brunei was willing to part with his 282-foot, $100 million yacht for a mere $30 million, he grabbed it. Trump's floating palace includes a swimming pool, 15 suites and a disco. He will spend an additional $2 million to dredge a channel so he can park the vessel next to his Atlantic City casino. While the 41-year-old billionaire may use the yacht as a retreat from his skyscraping empire in New York, if he ever feels out of touch he won't have far to go. There are 298 telephones on board and a heliport on deck.

Senate rejects Bork for Court 58 to 42

Oct 23. The fight is over. Judge Robert H. Bork has lost the battle to become a Supreme Court justice, as the Senate overwhelmingly rejected President Reagan's nominee by a vote of 58-42, the biggest margin of rejection of a Supreme Court nomination in the nation's history.

The nomination failure is a stinging defeat for the president, who had hoped Judge Bork would have tipped the ideological balance to the right on the high court.

The retirement of moderate Justice Lewis Powell this summer opened a seat on the court. Reagan seized the opportunity to select a conservative judge. But the Senate rejected Bork because his outspoken right-wing legal views were seen as too extreme for the court.

Upon hearing of the rejection, the president said, "I am saddened that the Senate has bowed today to a campaign of political pressure." He also vowed to find a nominee who would upset the Senate majority "just as much" as Bork did. This remark angered many lawmakers and prompted Sen. Edward Kennedy to say, "If we receive a nominee who thinks like Judge Bork, who opposes civil rights and civil liberties like Judge Bork, he will be rejected like Judge Bork." Administration aides have yet to say who will be the next nominee (→ 29).

Record lottery won as market crashes

Oct 19. At least two people in the United States don't give a hoot about the stock market tumble. Donald Woomer and Linda Despot are the happy recipients today of the largest lottery prize ever awarded in North America: $46 million. The couple hold the winning ticket in Pennsylvania's Super 7 game. Woomer, 55, and Despot, 37, an unmarried couple from Hollidaysburg, Pa., have no immediate plans for spending their fortune, but they have implied that there are some debts they will take care of. Despot will quit her job bookkeeping for a car dealer, and Woomer, a self-employed plasterer, will give himself an indefinite leave of absence.

Crash! Market plunges 508 points, exceeds 1929

Oct 20. The bottom fell out of the stock market yesterday, and no one knows for sure what will happen next. Wall Street had its worst day ever, far worse than 1929. The Dow Jones industrial average plummeted a record 508 points, closing at 1,738.74. Volume was an unprecedented 604 million shares, and the ticker fell two hours behind. The collapse sent shockwaves around the world. The Tokyo exchange opened down sharply this morning, and the Hong Kong market has closed for a week.

The Chairman of the New York Stock Exchange compared the market collapse to a nuclear accident. "It's the nearest thing to a meltdown that I ever want to see," John Phelan Jr. said. The Dean of the New York University business school said it was "a little like seeing the atom bomb go off. Once you've seen it," Richard West told The New York Times, "you know it could happen again. The world has changed."

Everyone from the small investor to the network anchorman is searching for villains. There appear to be many. Analysts blame the enormous budget and trade deficits, the falling dollar, rising interest rates and the latest tensions in the Persian Gulf. They also blame Wall Street itself and program trading. Arbitrageurs use the technique when they trade large blocks of stock to profit on the difference between their cash values and futures contracts. "They can't stop the selling once it gets going," one investor said. "It's just computers selling to computers. It became a gamble, not an investment any more."

It was a gamble that hurt millions of Americans. "People have been bloodied," economist Paul Samuelson said. Those with the biggest scars are the investors who watched $500 billion vanish from their portfolios. Workers planning to retire soon saw their savings shrink. Those who are still working have new concerns about losing their jobs. Businesses may cut back production, and economist Henry Kaufman warns that some of them may start laying employees off.

Despite all the gloom on Wall Street, some investors are still optimistic. They think stocks are a bargain, and today they rushed to buy the blue chips. This "flight to quality" pumped the Dow back up more than 100 points today, but it did not save the rest of the market. The stocks of many smaller companies are still in a free fall. No one wants them, and the number of loser stocks far outnumbered gainers.

One man who does not invest in stocks thinks there may be a lesson in what happened. "Maybe it will take the excessive greed out of things for a while," he said. And a retired Wall Street worker said, "All those guys with 65 credit cards and Porsches who think they are all geniuses at 25, now they see what's happened" (→ 21).

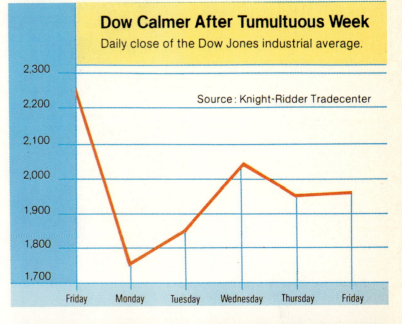

Dow Calmer After Tumultuous Week
Daily close of the Dow Jones industrial average.
Source: Knight-Ridder Tradecenter

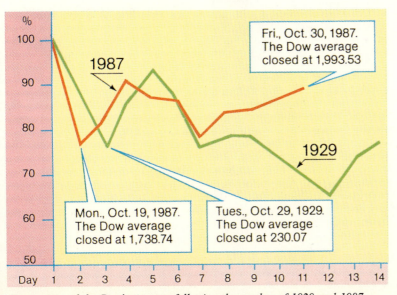

Comparison of the Dow's progress following the crashes of 1929 and 1987.

Fri., Oct. 30, 1987. The Dow average closed at 1,993.53

Mon., Oct. 19, 1987. The Dow average closed at 1,738.74

Tues., Oct. 29, 1929. The Dow average closed at 230.07

Market decline almost doubles 1929 figure

Oct 19. Older investors will never forget 1929, and some of them worry that history is repeating itself. When the Dow Jones industrial average dropped more than 500 points today, it lost 22.6 percent of its value. That is almost double the 12.82 percent decline on October 28, 1929.

Some analysts compare today's plunge to the 1929 collapse, which ushered in the Great Depression. The market boomed in the Roaring Twenties, and it boomed again in the eighties. In both decades, debt was high, relations with trading partners became strained, and parts of the economy were weak.

Many economists fear the decline in the market will accelerate a recession, but few seem to think there will be another depression. Most of the economy is still very strong, and unemployment and inflation both remain fairly low. Analysts also point out that safeguards have been built into the system to prevent aftershocks like the ones in 1929.

Wall Street does face a major new threat: the volatility of world markets. New York is now linked by computers to a global market, and stocks change hands around the clock. Nervousness by foreign traders and investors could make things even worse on Wall Street.

Su	Mo	Tu	We	Th	Fr	Sa
				1	2	3
4	5	6	7	8	9	10
11	12	13	14	15	16	17
18	19	20	21	22	23	24
25	26	27	28	29	30	31

26. Washington: Reagan bans all Iranian imports, curbs exports.

26. Hong Kong: Stock market, reopening first time in week, loses one-third of value (→ 27).

26. U.S.: Shere Hite publishes "Women and Love," claiming 84% of women "not satisfied emotionally" with romance.

27. St. Louis: Evidence indicates teenager died of AIDS in 1969, proving disease came to U.S. before 1980's epidemic (→ 12/10).

27. Seoul: Voters approve direct vote for president; Kim Dae Jung declares candidacy, splitting opposition (→ 12/16).

27. N.Y.: U.N. warns Reagan it faces insolvency if U.S. fails to pay dues this year (→ 11/23).

27. Washington: Navaho tribe and Oleg Cassini embark on joint venture to build luxury tourist resort on reservation.

27. U.S.: IBM, joining trend since market crash, announces $1 billion stock buyback (→ 27).

27. New York: Viyacheslav Zaitsev introduces fashion line in first retail licensing venture between U.S. and Soviets.

28. San Jose: Costa Rican President Arias urges Ortega to negotiate with contras (→ 11/2).

29. Las Vegas: Thomas "Hit Man" Hearns KO's Juan Roldan in middleweight bout, becoming first to win titles in four weight categories.

29. U.S.: Anti-Defamation League reports violent youth gangs called "skinheads" are terrorizing major cities.

30. Jerusalem: Israeli inquiry charges security officials systematically lied in trials to ensure conviction of terrorists (→ 12/15).

30. Mozambique: Govt. announces rebels killed 211 civilians in recent ambush (→ 11/6).

30. Fort Lauderdale, Fla.: Theresa Jackson convicted of child abuse in suicide of daughter she forced to work as stripper.

DEATHS

28. Andre Masson, French Surrealist painter (*1/4/1896).

29. Woody Herman, clarinetist, big band leader (*5/16/1913).

Dow rises 91 points; dollar still falling

Harried workers take calls in Hong Kong, where the market fell 33 percent.

Oct 30. The jitters on Wall Street have not disappeared yet, but the market calmed down yesterday and the Dow Jones industrial average was up more than 90 points. It closed at 1,938.33. That is 200 points higher than its close after the crash on the 19th. In addition to the gains for the blue chips, many smaller stocks also showed improvement. They climbed despite a further deterioration of the dollar. One analyst said, "The panic is being squeezed out of the market."

Not so this week in world markets. Tokyo stocks are lower, and Hong Kong started the week with a 33 percent decline.

Some observers say the administration and the Federal Reserve cannot do it all: calm Wall Street, prevent the economy from falling into a recession, keep interest rates low and let the dollar slide. If the dollar falls even lower, foreign investors could bail out of the market. Higher interest rates would attract foreign capital, but slow down the economy when it needs a boost.

On another front, many American firms are taking advantage of the decline in the market by buying back much of their stock. IBM says it is purchasing a billion dollars worth. Hundreds of other companies are following suit (→ 11/2).

Oct 25. Minnesota's Dan Gladden, after hitting a grand slam in the first game of the World Series. The Twins won their first Series tonight, beating St. Louis 4-2 in the last game before a record crowd of hanky-waving fans.

Losing investor kills stockbroker

Oct 27. A distraught investor who killed a stockbroker before killing himself was leading a double life in Miami. The man known to co-workers at a Social Security office in Miami as Arthur Kane actually was Arthur H. Katz, a Kansas City lawyer who was convicted a decade ago in a mail fraud scheme. After serving six months in jail, he was enrolled in the federal witness protection program and given a new identity. However, officials said there was no indication that his past had anything to do with the murder and suicide, which took place in a Merrill Lynch office after the stock market plunged (→ 30).

Study claims twenty million underfed

Oct 26. Americans go hungry every day. That's the conclusion reached by the Physician's Task Force on Hunger in America in a report released today. According to the study, 20 million citizens are underfed. The chief researcher of the study, Harvard Health Professor Larry Brown, blames the Reagan administration. "I think the main point that we draw is that supply-side economics has failed as a remedy for hunger," he said.

Treehouse builder is called a slumlord

Oct 27. When his 16-year-old son ran away from home, Mark Tucker felt guilty. He'd never been the proper father, never made good on his promises—one of which was to build a treehouse. So he built one—a glorious, multi-level edifice on a grand spreading tree. And his son, truly touched, came home. However, the town of St. Louis Park, Minnesota, said Tucker's treehouse failed to conform to building codes and threatened to bulldoze it. Then the city accused him of being the landlord of some rat-infested apartments (real ones, not in trees). Slumlord Tucker will serve jail time next month. Hopefully, his son will visit often.

Reagan picks Ginsburg as Court candidate

Ginsburg, a second try for Reagan.

Oct 29. President Reagan nominated Judge Douglas Ginsburg today to fill the vacancy on the Supreme Court. However, the selection is expected to face a similar battle to the one waged against Judge Robert H. Bork, the president's first choice to fill the court seat left empty when Justice Lewis Powell resigned this summer. The Bork nomination was rejected by the Senate last week.

Several Democratic Senators told the Reagan administration that Ginsburg was the most controversial of all the candidates on the White House list. Despite this warning, the president chose the conservative judge from the U.S. District Court of Appeals for the Ninth Circuit. Ginsburg is reportedly the favorite choice of Attorney General Edwin Meese.

President Reagan said his nominee is "a believer in judicial restraint" and is tough on law and order issues, two criteria important to the administration. Early critics of the selection feel Ginsburg is inexperienced; he has served only 14 months as a judge (→ 11/5).

Human rights advocate is slain in Salvador

Oct 26. While his two children watched in horror, Herbert Ernesto Anaya was murdered today in San Salvador. Two gunmen waited for the Salvadoran human rights commission chief to take his children to school. As he started to get into his car, the assassins crept up and fired at point-blank range, leaving Anaya dead in a pool of blood.

No group or individuals have claimed responsibility for the political assassination, but a spokesman for the human rights commission, Miguel Angel Montenegro, believes El Salvador's right-wing military death squads are to blame. Anaya is the fourth human rights panel member killed since 1980 in this volatile nation.

A government spokesman said, "This irrational act reflects the level of hate and rancor that exists in the hearts and minds of some Salvadorans." According to Anaya's father, the human rights leader had a premonition he would be a target for murder (→ 11/15).

Blood stains the pavement at the site of Anaya's assassination.

Gorbachev to meet Reagan in the U.S.

Oct 30. President Reagan will get the chance to play host to Mikhail Gorbachev in December, but it will not be a long party. The president announced today that he and the Soviet leader will begin a short summit meeting on December 7. They are expected to sign a treaty banning short- and medium-range nuclear missiles.

Reagan was hoping that Gorbachev would turn the visit into a grand tour and even visit his California ranch. Soviet officials turned down the invitation by saying that Gorbachev's security would be threatened. It is widely believed, however, that the Soviet leader does not want to do anything that might improve the political standing of a lame-duck administration. Gorbachev also faces opposition at home to the nuclear treaty (→ 11/20).

Filipino guerrillas kill two U.S. airmen

Oct 28. In a series of incidents near Clark Air Base in the Philippines, two American airmen, as well as two other men, were shot and killed. Although local residents seemed to suspect that the attacks were the work of right-wing forces who have recently sought to destabilize the government, Philippine officials said that the killings were in the style of Communist guerrillas.

Woody Herman, big band leader, dies

Oct 29. Woody Herman, the eclectic and enduring big band leader and virtuoso on the clarinet, died today at 74. Herman's ability to organize and direct musicians kept his sound alive from the 1930's until his last album in 1986. Herman and his Thundering Herd toured religiously, playing everywhere from Carnegie Hall to rock auditoriums to Vegas clubs. "Every night a new club," he said. Right up until Herman's death, he was deluged with requests for his 1939 hit, "Woodchoppers' Ball."

Titan flies, ending two years of failure

Titan 34D: a military payload.

Oct 26. A two-year string of space failures ended when the Air Force successfully launched a Titan 34D rocket carrying a top-secret spy satellite. The Titan, America's most powerful unmanned rocket, had been grounded after successive launch failures in 1985 and 1986.

Today's successful launch took place at Vandenberg Air Force Base in California and was described as having "tremendous significance for the nation's space program" by Air Force Secretary Edward C. Aldridge Jr. While the Air Force gave no information on the payload, experts said it was a KH-11 reconnaissance satellite, the most sophisticated available, essential for monitoring any of the arms control agreements now being negotiated with the Soviets (→ 11/4).

Oct 25. NFL regulars are back, first time since the strike. Above: Browns linebacker Chip Banks.

1,500 perish as Philippine ferry sinks

The 2,150-ton ferry Dona Paz in the harbor before her fateful voyage.

Dec 21. Early today, 110 miles south of Manila, rescuers searched under flame-lit skies for some 1,500 people presumed lost in the worst maritime disaster in 39 years. A grim tale has been told by 26 survivors, most of them badly burned.

The ferry Dona Paz was terribly overcrowded on its way from Mindoro island to Manila. Its register lists 1,493 passengers, but survivors say there may have been as many as 3,000. At 10 p.m., with some sleeping four to a cot on deck, the ferry struck a 629-ton Philippine oil tanker. Fire spread quickly and both ships went down within minutes. Virtually no debris has been found, said a Coast Guard spokesman, suggesting "most of the passengers went down with the ship."

The worst modern disaster at sea occurred in 1945 when a Soviet sub sank a Nazi ship evacuating Germans from Poland; 7,700 died. Some 6,000 died off Manchuria in 1948 during the evacuation of Yingkow, and 3,920 refugees were lost off Shanghai the next month. The Titanic disaster of 1912 took more than 1,500 lives, and 1,198 died on the Lusitania in 1915.

"Squeaky" snared

Dec 26. Lynette "Squeaky" Fromme has been recaptured. The follower of mass murderer Charles Manson escaped two days ago from the West Virginia prison where she is serving a life sentence for trying to kill ex-President Ford. She was a model inmate, although she was transferred there after attacking a fellow inmate with a hammer.

Santas suspended

Dec 21. In most places, Santa is met with merriment. Not so at the Okonite cable plant in North Brunswick, New Jersey, where 100 workers were suspended for showing up in Santa hats. Plant officials said they were "carnival-like headwear ... not appropriate for a business environment." The workers called their manager "Scrooge."

Racial case ends in manslaughter

Dec 21. After twelve days of deliberation, a jury has found three white teenagers guilty of manslaughter for the death of a black man in Howard Beach, Queens. Michael Griffith died a year ago when a gang of youths chased him into the path of an onrushing car.

The case has stirred racial tensions in New York, and the verdict angered many blacks who felt the youths should have been found guilty of murder. Those upset with the manslaughter conviction organized a massive protest in the city's subway system, disrupting service at the height of the rush hour. When the verdict was read, three protesters were dragged from the courtroom, yelling, "Murderers!" Mayor Ed Koch called the verdict "fair and reasonable."

1987: Biggest year in movies in memory

This was a year in which more movies were released than at any time in memory, and many of these were exceptionally good. Michael Douglas starred in "Fatal Attraction," a thriller about romantic obsession, and "Wall Street," a timely, moralistic look at business. "America has become a second-rate power," warns Gordon Gekko (Douglas), a corporate raider, and greed is what will make it great again. Oliver Stone directed.

Vietnam was the focus of at least five films, including "Platoon" (also directed by Stone), Stanley Kubrick's "Full Metal Jacket," and "Good Morning, Vietnam," with comedian Robin Williams as an unconventional radio announcer.

Spielberg's "Empire of the Sun."

William Hurt played an anchorman in "Broadcast News," a comedy filled with satiric thrusts at the shallowness of TV journalism. "Walker" was an offbeat look at Americans scheming in Nicaragua in the 1850's. And "The Untouchables" starred Robert DeNiro.

It was a big year for the historical epic. Both Bernardo Bertolucci's "The Last Emperor" and Steven Spielberg's "Empire of the Sun" focused on 20th-Century China.

Douglas, Glenn Close: "Fatal" stars.

Books warn of educational, economic woes

Two controversial books this year put the spotlight on American education, which has come under fire of late. "The Closing of the American Mind," by Allan Bloom, blames America's democratic culture for a decline in educational standards and performance. Bloom seems to think that only education for the few will save the nation from inevitable decay. "Cultural Literacy: What Every American Needs to Know," by E.D. Hirsch Jr., attributes our "ignorance of cultural history to the progressive movement in education." The book also includes a list of 63 pages of what an educated person should know.

The most provocative book of the year has to be "The Great Depression of 1990," by Dr. Ravi Batra. Applying a cyclical theory of history to our immediate future, Batra concludes that the eighties parallel the twenties and we are headed for an inevitable economic depression. According to this economist, depressions are caused by a concentration of wealth in the hands of the privileged few. He offers advice on ways to avoid being hit by the coming catastrophe.

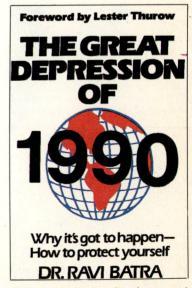

Foreword by Lester Thurow
THE GREAT DEPRESSION OF 1990
Why it's got to happen—How to protect yourself
DR. RAVI BATRA

Visionary or just another doomsayer?

The World's Nations

This section gives brief updated facts on each nation's geographical location, population, area, language, religion, political status, and membership in international organizations. The head of state and head of government are also named. Figures provided for Gross National Product (GNP) and population are the latest available. Currency values are based on November 27, 1987, indicative rates. The texts provide a short summary of the main events of 1987. A list of abbreviations used is provided on page 123.

Afghanistan

Central Asia
251,773 sq. mi.
Pop. : 15,056,000
UN

Capital : Kabul (Pop. : 1,400,000)
Official languages : Pashta, Dari Persian
Religion : Moslem (Shiite 20 %, Sunni 80 %)
Political status : People's republic
Head of state : Najibullah (since 1986)
Head of government : Sultan Ali Keshtmand (since 1981)
GNP : $ 3.5 bil. (1984)
Currency : Afghani ($ 1 US = 50.60)

Despite a new and massive vote at the United Nations in November calling for a Soviet pullout (123 for, 19 against and 11 abstentions), the situation on the ground remained stalemated. An estimated 115,000 Soviet troops, which invaded the country in December 1979, continued to suffer losses both in men and materiel. In all, over 20,000 Soviet troops are believed to have died in the war, while more than five million Afghans have fled the country. In mid-summer, Soviet forces backed by Afghan soldiers were forced to withdraw from several exposed bases because improved rebel anti-aircraft defenses made re-supply difficult. Western experts said that U.S.-supplied Stinger anti-aircraft missiles had become a major element in the Mujahedeen's arsenal, leading to a decline in the use of aircraft by Soviet forces. The main Afghan guerrilla groups remained firm in their rejection of Kabul's national reconciliation policy put forward since early 1987 by the pro-Soviet regime. Rebel leaders refused to recognize what they see as the Soviet " puppet regime " in Kabul. In October, Maulawi Mohammed Yunus Khales was named chief of the seven-party Afghan resistance alliance. In September, Afghan Communist Party leader Najibullah was formally confirmed as the country's president. He had been running the country's affairs since taking over as party secretary general in May 1986 from Babrak Karmal. Yunus Khales met in Washington with President Reagan who pledged continued support. Moscow in September offered to pull out its troops over a 12-month period conditioned on the temporary establishment of a coali-

tion dominated by the Afghan Communist Party, but the U.S. rejected this. At the U.S.-Soviet summit meeting in December, no breakthroughs were reported on the withdrawal of Soviet troops from Afghanistan.

Albania

Southeastern
Europe
11,100 sq. mi.
Pop : 3,070,000
UN

Capital : Tirana (Pop. : 272,000)
Official language : Albanian
Religions : officially atheist; mostly Moslem
Political status : Socialist people's republic
Head of state : Ramiz Alia (since 1982)
Head of government : Adil Carcani (since 1982)
GNP : $2.5 bil. (1984)
Currency : Lek ($ 1 US = 5.62)

The state of war between Albania and Greece, in force since October 28, 1940, was formally lifted on August 28, after a joint decision taken in 1985.

Algeria

North Africa
918,497 sq. mi.
Pop. : 22,600,000
UN, AL, OAU, OPEC

Capital : Algiers (Pop. : 2,200,000)
Official language : Arabic
Religion : Sunni Moslem
Political status : Socialist republic
Head of state : Chadli Bendjedid (since 1979)
Head of government : Abdel Hamid Brahimi (since 1984)
GNP : $57 bil (1986)
Currency : Algerian dinar ($ 1 US = 4.67)

Four Moslem fundamentalists were sentenced to death in July for conspiracy and assassination, in Algeria's biggest trial since its 1962 independence. In November, the U.S. promised a $600 million aid package.

Andorra

Southern
Europe
188 sq. mi.
Pop. : 42,712

Capital : Andorra la Vella
Official language : Catalan
Religion : Roman Catholic
Political status : Principality
Heads of state : The Spanish bishop of Urgel, Mgr. Joan Marti y Alanis, and French President François Mitterrand
Head of government : Josef Pintat Solans (since 1986)
GNP : $9,000 per capita
Currency : French franc and Spanish peseta

Angola

Southwestern
Africa
481,353 sq. mi.
Pop. : 8,960,000
UN, OAU

Capital : Luanda (Pop. : 960,000)
Official language : Portuguese
Religions : Roman Catholic 46 %, Protestant 12 %, animist 42 %
Political status : Socialist people's republic
Head of state : Jose E. dos Santos (since 1979)
Head of government : Jose E. dos Santos (since 1979)
GNP : $6.9 bil. (1984)
Currency : Kwanza ($ 1 US = 29.92)

Strife-torn Marxist Angola continued to be rocked by attacks from the South African and U.S.-backed UNITA rebels, as U.S. diplomats worked to get a withdrawal of the estimated 40,000 Cuban troops. UNITA claimed to control a third of Angola. The war brought further economic disarray. In June, a U.S. pilot was freed after being held for violating Angolan airspace. South African and UNITA forces launched a major November offensive in the south. South African forces pulled out in December after fierce fighting. Efforts to end the war stalled on Angola's insistence that Cuban troops would pull out only if South Africa ended its occupation of neighboring Namibia.

Antigua and Barbuda

Caribbean
171 sq. mi.
Pop. : 81,500
UN, OAS, Caricom, CW

Capital : St. John's (Pop. : 25,000)
Official language : English
Religion : Anglican (85 %)
Political status : Constitutional monarchy
Head of state : Queen Elizabeth II
Head of government : Vere C.Bird (since 1981)
GNP : $150 mil. (1984)
Currency : East Caribbean dollar ($ 1 US = 2.70)

Argentina

South America
1,065,189 sq. mi.
Pop. : 31,060,000
UN, LAIA, OAS

Capital : Buenos Aires (Pop. : 3,000,000)
Official language : Spanish
Religion : Roman Catholic 92 %
Political status : Federal republic
Head of state : Raul Alfonsin (since 1983)
Head of government : Raul Alfonsin (since 1983)
GNP : $60.6 bil. (1985)
Currency : Austral ($ 1 US = 3.50)

President Alfonsin's ruling party suffered a September election setback, as the opposition Peronists gained seats. Mr. Alfonsin postponed constitutional reform plans and said he sought a negotiated settlement of the country's $54 billion foreign debt. The government vowed in November to let private industry compete with state-run firms in all sectors except oil. The army's chain of command survived a mutiny by an infantry regiment. The long-running sovereignty dispute with Britain over the Falklands remained stalemated. In mid-September, Argentina signed an anti-drug cooperation pact with the U.S.

Australia

South Pacific
2,966,200 sq. mi.
Pop. : 15,450,000
UN, ANZUS,
CW,
OECD

Capital : Canberra
(Pop. : 264,000)
Official language : English
Religions : Anglican 36 %, other Protestant
25 %, Roman Catholic 33 %
Political status : Federal constitutional
monarchy
Head of state : Queen Elizabeth II
Head of government : Robert James Lee
Hawke (since 1983)
GNP : $161.4 bil. (1986)
Currency : Australian dollar
($ 1 US = 1.44)

Premier Bob Hawke's Labor Party
won a historic third consecutive term
in July elections, capitalizing on disu-
nity in opposition ranks. In May, the
government showed concern at increased Libyan activity in the South
Pacific, saying this could destabilize
the region. A September visit by a
large U.S. Navy fleet sparked anti-
U.S. demonstrations. Veteran politician Sir Joh Bjelke-Petersen, premier
of Queensland for 20 years, retired in
October. A Royal Commission in
November reported that at least 64
aborigines had died in jail or police
custody since 1979. November figures
showed a drop in the net foreign debt.

Austria

Western Europe
32,374 sq. mi.
Pop : 7,550,000
UN, EFTA, EC,
OECD

Capital : Vienna (Pop. : 1,500,000)
Official language : German
Religion : Roman Catholic 85 %
Political status : Federal parliamentary
and democratic republic
Head of state : Kurt Waldheim (since
1986)
Head of government : Franz Vranitzky
(since 1986)
GNP : $94 bil. (1986)
Currency : Schilling ($ 1 US = 11.71)

President Waldheim was effectively
barred by Washington in April from
entry into the United States, after
charges that he took part in Nazi war
crimes. Austrians reacted angrily to
the move, but Mr. Waldheim said he
believed he would be crossed off the
" undesirable " list after the 1988 U.S.
presidential elections. Austrian Jews
called on the government to halt what
they saw as an alarming rise in anti-
Semitism spurred by Jewish attacks
against Mr. Waldheim. In November,
Michael Graff, the deputy leader of a
conservative party resigned following
the publication of anti-Semitic
remarks.

Bahamas

Caribbean
5,380 sq. mi.
Pop. : 235,000
UN, OAS, CW,
OECD

Capital : Nassau (Pop. : 140,000)
Official language : English
Religions : Baptist 29 %, Anglican 23 %,
Roman Catholic 22 %
Political status : Constitutional
monarchy
Head of state : Queen Elizabeth II
Head of government : Lynden O.Pindling
(since 1967)
GNP : $1.6 bil. (1985)
Currency : Bahamian dollar
($ 1 US = 1)

Premier Sir Lynden Pindling, 57, was
reelected in June national elections
for a fifth five-year term. Reports of
a tiny Bahamian island being used as
a transit point for U.S.-bound drugs
continued.

Bahrain

Middle East
258 sq. mi.
Pop. : 435,065
UN, AL, GCC

Capital : Manama (Pop.: 108,700)
Official language : Arabic
Religion : Moslem (Sunni 40 %, Shiite
60 %)
Political status : Emirate
Head of state : Isa bin Sulman Al Khalifa
(since 1961)
Head of government : Khalifa bin Sulman
Al Khalifa (since 1973)
GNP : $4.1 bil. (1985)
Currency : Bahrain dinar ($ 1 US = 0.37)

U.S. Defense Secretary Caspar Weinberger in a September visit discussed
joint military cooperation. In January, Washington said it would sell
Bahrain a $400 million arms package.

Bangladesh

Southern Asia
55,598 sq. mi.
Pop. :
101,720,000
UN, CW

Capital : Dhaka (Pop. : 3,500,000)
Official language : Bengali
Religions : Moslem 86 %, Hindu 12 %
Political status : Presidential republic
Head of state : Hussain Mohammad
Ershad (since 1983)
Head of government : Mizanur Rahman
Chowdhury (since 1986)
GNP : $17 bil. (1986)
Currency : Taka ($ 1 US = 31.10)

September floods killed over 1,500
people and caused further problems
for the strained economy. Nationwide
opposition-led strikes erupted in November protests aimed at ousting the
Ershad government and several people were reported killed.

Barbados

Caribbean
166 sq. mi.
Pop. : 253,055
UN, CW,
Caricom, OAS

Capital : Bridgetown (Pop. : 7,500)
Official language : English
Religions : Anglican 70 %, Methodist 9 %,
Roman Catholic 4 %
Political status : Constitutional monarchy
Head of state : Queen Elizabeth II
Head of government : Erskine Sandiford
(since 06/01/87)
GNP : $1.1 bil. (1984)
Currency : Barbados dollar
($ 1 US = 2.01)

Belgium

Western Europe
11,779 sq.mi.
Pop. : 9,860,000
UN, EEC, EC,
NATO, OECD

Capital : Brussels (Pop. : 1,000,000)
Official languages : French, Dutch,
German
Religion : Roman Catholic 96 %
Political status : Constitutional monarchy
Head of state : King Baudouin I (since
1951)
Head of government : Wilfried Martens
(since 1981)
GNP : $76.3 bil. (1984)
Currency : Belgian franc ($ 1 US = 35.50)

Premier Wilfried Martens, in power
since 1981, resigned after a December
election setback. The center-right ruling coalition suffered losses to the
opposition socialist parties, and socialist politician Willy Claes, 49, was
likely to be Belgium's new premier.

Belize

Central America
8,867 sq. mi.
Pop. : 166,200
UN, Caricom,
CW

Capital : Belmopan (Pop. : 8,000)
Official language : English
Religions : Roman Catholic 66 %,
Methodist 13 %, Anglican 13 %
Political status : Constitutional monarchy
Head of state : Queen Elizabeth II

Head of government : Manuel A.
Esquivel (since 1985)
GNP : $180 mil. (1985)
Currency : Belize dollar ($ 1 US = 2)

Benin

West Africa
43,483 sq. mi.
Pop. : 4,142,000
UN, ECOWAS,
OAU

Capital : Porto Novo (Pop. : 208,000)
Official language : French
Religions : Mainly animist with
Christian, Moslem minorities
Political status : Socialist people's
republic
Head of state : Mathieu Kerekou (since
1972)
Head of government : Mathieu Kerekou
(since 1972)
GNP : $1.02 bil. (1985)
Currency : CFA franc ($ 1 US = 282.55)

Bhutan

South Asia
18,147 sq. mi.
Pop. : 1,300,000
UN

Capital : Thimphu (Pop. : 20,000)
Official language : Dzongkha
Religions : Buddhist 75 %, Hindu 25 %,
Moslem 5 %
Political status : Monarchy
Head of state : Jigme Singye Wangchuk
(since 1972)
Head of government : Council of
ministers
GNP : $190 mil. (1985)
Currency : Ngultrum ($ 1 US = 12.97)

Bolivia

South America
424,165 sq. mi.
Pop. : 6,252,250
UN, LAIA,
OAS

Capital : Sucre (legal), La Paz (de facto;
pop. : 916,000)
Official languages : Spanish, Quechua
Religion : Roman Catholic 95 %
Political status : Presidential republic
Head of state : Victor Paz Estenssoro
(since 1985)
Head of government : Victor Paz
Estenssoro
GNP : $3.1 bil. (1985)
Currency : Bolivian peso
($ 1 US = 2.15)

Anti-cocaine operations were stepped
up and growers were offered rewards
to switch to other crops. In August,
there was labor unrest, but the government won its fight against runaway inflation.

Botswana

Southern Africa
231,804 sq. mi.
Pop. : 1,050,200
UN, CW, OAU

Capital : Gaborone (Pop. : 70,000)
Official languages : English, Tswana
Religions : indigenous beliefs (majority),
Christian 15 %
Political status : Presidential republic
Head of state : Quett Masire
(since 1980)
Head of government : Quett Masire
GNP : $950 mil. (1986)
Currency : Pula ($ 1 US = 1.61)

Brazil

South America
3,286,470 sq. mi.
Pop. :
138,403,000
UN, LAIA,
OAS

Capital : Brasilia (Pop. : 1,200,000)
Official language : Portuguese
Religion : Roman Catholic 89 %
Political status : Federal republic
Head of state : Jose Sarney
(since 1985)
Head of government : Jose Sarney
GNP : $222 bil. (1985)
Currency : Cruzeiro
($ 1 US = 60.97)

With a foreign debt of over $112 bil-
lion, the world's biggest, Brazil in
February suspended its debt
payments, but said later it would seek
to work out a plan allowing resump-
tion of interest and principal
payments. In September, Brazil pre-
sented a new plan to restructure its
$70 billion debt to commercial len-
ders, but called for fresh credits to pay
interest accumulated since the February suspension. Raging inflation
and popular discontent continued to
place the country's two-year-old democracy under heavy stress. President
Sarney came under fire for his economic policies and there were growing
calls for early elections. Bitterness
spread and there were violent clashes
in the capital. In late 1987, a new
constitution was drafted, and the text
raised political tensions, promising to
make 1988 a watershed year for the
young democracy. Leftist groups, led
by labor unions, sought to block
efforts by conservatives to change
liberal social measures included in the
draft constitution. In Rio de Janeiro,
the year was marked by an orgy of
killings, as " death squads," or
groups of off-duty policemen, shot it
out with gangsters and drug traffickers. In six months, " death squads "
were said to have killed over
1,000 people in the former capital. At
least four died after a September
radioactive leak, caused when a junk
dealer opened a radiotherapy
machine.

Brunei

Southeast Asia
2,226 sq. mi.
Pop. : 221,900
UN, CW,
ASEAN

Capital : Bandar Seri Begawan
(Pop. : 75,000)
Official language : Malay
Religions : Moslem 64 %, Buddhist 14 %,
Christian 10 %
Political status : Sultanate
Head of state : Sultan Muda Hassanal
Bolkiah Muizzadin Waddaulah (since
1967)
Head of government : Sultan Muda
Hassanal Bolkiah Muizzadin Waddaulah
GNP : $3.1 bil. (1985)
Currency : Brunei dollar
($ 1 US = 2.03)

Bulgaria

Southeastern
Europe
42,823 sq. mi.
Pop. : 8,943,000
UN, CMEA,
Warsaw Pact

Capital : Sofia (Pop. : 1,100,000)
Official language : Bulgarian
Religions : Orthodox 85 %, Moslem 13 %
Political status : Socialist people's
republic
Head of state : Todor Zhivkov (since
1971)
Head of government : Georgi Atanasov
(since 1986)
GNP : $52 bil. (1984)
Currency : Lev ($ 1 US = 0.85)

Burkina Faso

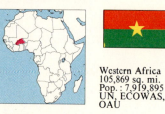

Western Africa
105,869 sq. mi.
Pop. : 7,919,895
UN, ECOWAS,
OAU

Capital : Ouagadougou
(Pop. : 360,000)
Official language : French
Religions : animist 50 %, Moslem 16 %,
Roman Catholic 8 %
Political status : Presidential republic
Head of state : Blaise Compaoré (since
10/15/87)
Head of government : Blaise Compaoré
(since 10/15/87)
GNP : $1.08 bil. (1985)
Currency : CFA franc
($ 1 US = 282.55)

In a bloody October coup, Burkinabe
leader Thomas Sankara was overthrown and killed by his second in
command, Captain Blaise Compaoré,
who named himself president and
premier; 12 of Capt. Sankara's aides
died in the coup.

Burma

Southeast Asia
261,789 sq. mi.
Pop. : 36,919,000
UN

Capital : Rangoon (Pop. : 3,500,000)
Official language : Burmese
Religions : Buddhist 85 %, animist,
Christian
Political status : Socialist people's republic
Head of state : U San Yu (since 1981)
Head of government : U Maung Maung
Kha (since 1977)
GNP : $7.07 bil. (1985)
Currency : Kyat ($ 1 US = 6.33)

Burmese leader Ne Win in September
stunned the nation by declaring the
three highest banknotes valueless in a
bid to curb black marketeers who
sparked student riots.

Burundi

Central Africa
10,759 sq. mi.
Pop. : 4,923,000
UN, OAU

Capital : Bujumbura (Pop. : 250,000)
Official languages : French, Rundi
Religions : Roman Catholic 62 %,
traditional African 32 %
Political status : Presidential republic
Head of state : Pierre Buyoya (since
9/9/87)
Head of government : Pierre Buyoya
(since 9/9/87)
GNP : $1.02 bil. (1986)
Currency : Burundi franc
($ 1 US = 118.59)

Cambodia

Southeast Asia
69,898 sq. mi.
Pop. : 6,232,000
UN

Capital : Phnom Penh (Pop. : 500,000)
Official language : Khmer
Religions : Theravada Buddhism, animism
Political status : Democratic people's
republic
Head of state : Heng Samrin (since 1979)
Head of government : Hun Sen (since
1985)
GNP : $1.1 bil. (1984)
Currency : Riel ($ 1 US = 100)

Hopes for a breakthrough in the
nine-year Cambodian conflict were
boosted by a December meeting in
France between rival Cambodian leaders Hun Sen, backed by Hanoi, and
Prince Sihanouk. The landmark talks
did not however resolve the toughest

obstacles to peace. Both sides pledged
to seek a political solution to the war,
which has cost hundreds of thousands
of lives. But no mention was made of
the 140,000 Vietnamese troops in
Cambodia. There were hopes of further progress in 1988.

Cameroon

Western Central
Africa
185,568 sq. mi.
Pop. : 9,880,000
UN, OAU

Capital : Yaounde (Pop. : 580,000)
Official languages : French, English
Religions : Roman Catholic 35 %, animist
25 %, Moslem 22 %, Protestant 18 %
Political status : Presidential republic
Head of state : Paul Biya (since 1982)
Head of government : Paul Biya (since
1982)
GNP : $11.5 bil. (1986)
Currency : CFA franc
($ 1 US = 282.55)

Canada

North America
3,851,790 sq. mi.
Pop. : 25,591,000
UN, NATO,
OECD

Capital : Ottawa (Pop. : 717,000)
Official languages : English, French
Religions : Roman Catholic 46 %,
Protestant 41 %
Political status : Parliamentary monarchy
Head of state : Queen Elizabeth II
Head of government : Brian Mulroney
(since 1984)
GNP : $358.8 bil. (1986)
Currency : Canadian dollar
($ 1 US = 1.31)

It was an active year for the country
both at home and abroad. In April,
the government said Austrian President Kurt Waldheim would not be
welcome, in the wake of a move by
Washington to bar him from entry
into the U.S. These steps followed
charges that he had been involved in
Nazi war crimes. In March, Canada
announced it would withhold accredi-
tation from Gen. Amos Yaron, named as Israel's defense attache, after
he had been reprimanded in an official Israeli report on the 1982 massa-
cre of Palestinian civilians in Beirut.
In August, External Affairs Minister
Joe Clark threatened to sever diplomatic and economic ties with South
Africa if efforts to persuade Pretoria
to end apartheid failed. At a September meeting in Montreal, delegates
from some 40 nations approved a
treaty for the protection of the earth's
ozone layer, as the U.S. was held
accountable for 30 percent of the
ozone-destroying chemicals worldwide, while the 12-member EEC pro-

duced 48 percent. The September Francophone summit was marked by a multimillion dollar program to aid the movement's neediest members. At the summit, Canada said it would cancel nearly 250 million U.S. dollars owed by seven African nations. The French-speaking leaders represented some 300 million people. Two notable visitors came to Canada in 1987 : Queen Elizabeth II, who attended the Commonwealth Heads of Government meeting in Vancouver, traveled to Victoria, Saskatchewan and paid her first official visit to Montreal since 1976. President Mitterrand also toured the country, in the first visit by a French head of state since Gen. Charles de Gaulle's controversial 1967 trip. On the home front, the year's start was marked by Transport Minister André Bissonnette's dismissal from the Cabinet after an inquiry into a land deal. In June, Prime Minister Mulroney and ten provincial premiers signed the final version of the April Meech Lake accord redefining the character of Canada's federalism and recognizing the status of Quebec as a " distinct society " within Canada. On November 1, charismatic former Premier Rene Levesque, who symbolized Quebec's struggle for independence, died at 66 after a political career spanning 25 years. Calls for tougher measures against illegal immigration followed the July arrival of 174 Indians off the coast of Nova Scotia. A devastating summer tornado killed 35 in Edmonton, in the worst natural disaster to hit Canada since a 1954 hurricane left 81 dead. In Ottawa, a woman gave birth to quintuplets in September, apparently the first such birth in Canada since the five Dionne sisters attracted worldwide attention in 1934. In July, the socialist New Democratic Party won federal by-elections in Newfoundland, Yukon and Ontario. An August Cabinet reshuffle saw the replacement of the industry minister and major new powers were given to Mr. Mulroney's deputy. Despite progress, the long-awaited Canada-U.S. free trade agreement was still giving negotiators problems in December, as they struggled to agree on a final text. The vital accord was nonetheless due to be signed in January 1988 by Mr. Mulroney and President Reagan. The acid rain issue continued to mar Canada's relations with the Reagan administration. Late in the year, the pacifist and pro-ecology group Greenpeace launched a five-year campaign to block Canadian uranium exports to countries with nuclear weapons. On defense issues, it was decided to give priority over the next 15 years to modernizing Canada's navy, deploying surveillance satellites and upgrading military preparedness. In October, a new Canada-U.S. military radar alert system came into operation, scoring a first success with the interception of two Soviet air force planes north of Yukon province. The country's intelligence service underwent a November shake-up in a bid to restore flagging morale after charges from opposition parliamentarians that the service was confusing the legal right to dissent with threats to national security.

Cape Verde

Atlantic
1,750 sq. mi.
Pop. : 319,000
UN, ECOWAS,
OAU

Capital : Praia (Pop. : 40,000)
Official language : Portuguese
Religion : Roman Catholic 98 %
Political status : Republic
Head of state : Aristide Pereira (since 1975)
Head of government : Pedro Pires (since 1975)
GNP : $97 mil. (1986)
Currency : Cape Verde escudo ($ 1 US = 72.18)

Central African Republic

Central Africa
240,534 sq. mi.
Pop. : 2,700,000
UN, OAU

Capital : Bangui (Pop. : 473,000)
Official language : French
Religions : Protestant 25 %, Roman Catholic 25 %, traditional 24 %
Political status : Presidential republic
Head of state : Gen. André Kolingba (since 1981)
Head of government : Gen. André Kolingba (since 1981)
GNP : 660 mil. (1985)
Currency : CFA franc ($ 1 US = 282.55)

Chad

Central Africa
495,755 sq. mi.
Pop. : 5,120,000
UN, OAU

Capital : N'Djamena (Pop. : 300,000)
Official languages : French, Arabic
Religions : Moslem 44 %, animist 23 %, Christian 33 %
Political status : Presidential republic
Head of state : Hissen Habre (since 1982)
Head of government : Hissen Habre (since 1982)
GNP : $400 mil. (1985)
Currency : CFA franc ($ 1 US = 282.55)

Libyan forces in August recaptured the northern oasis town of Aouzou, after suffering stinging defeats earlier in the year. Chad officials said almost 7,000 Libyan soldiers had been killed or captured since the start of the year, and the value of equipment abandoned by fleeing Libyan troops was valued at several billion dollars. In September, Chadian forces destroyed a key military base in southeast Libya.

But the conflict severely strained Chad's limited economy, despite increased French support and U.S.-supplied Stinger anti-aircraft missiles. In September, a Soviet-built Libyan bomber was downed over Ndjamena, as Chad and Libya agreed to a cease-fire.

Chile

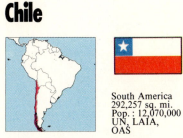

South America
292,257 sq. mi.
Pop. : 12,070,000
UN, LAIA, OAS

Capital : Santiago (Pop. : 3,900,000)
Official language : Spanish
Religions : Roman Catholic 79 %, Protestant 6 %
Political status : Presidential republic under a military regime
Head of state : Augusto Pinochet Ugarte (since 1973)
Head of government : Augusto Pinochet Ugarte (since 1973)
GNP : $16.8 bil. (1986)
Currency : Chilean peso ($ 1 US = 230.61)

On January 2, the government lifted a nighttime curfew in Santiago which had been enforced since President Pinochet's 1973 takeover. Gen. Pinochet also invited political exiles to return. The move was hailed by Washington. In August, U.S. Senators said Chile's human rights violations were affecting bilateral relations, while General Pinochet promised a presidential referendum in 1988 rather than 1989, and said he was confident his party would win another eight-year term. Leftist leaders stepped up calls for an anti-Pinochet vote. At least one person died and hundreds were arrested in violent clashes during an October general strike.

China

East Asia
3,691,795 sq. mi.
Pop. :
1,034,750,000
UN

Capital : Peking (Pop. : 9,500,000)
Official language : Chinese
Religions : officially atheist; Confucianism, Buddhism, Taoism
Political status : People's republic
Head of state : Li Xiannian (since 1983)
Head of government : Li Peng (since 11/24/1987)
GNP : $270 bil. (1985)
Currency : Renminbi Yuan ($ 1 US = 3.72)

China in 1987 underwent its most serious political crisis since the 1976 death of Mao Tse-tung. The country also carried out a major rejuvenation of the ageing Communist Party leadership, but the problem of finding a successor to 83-year-old Deng Hsiaoping was not resolved. A crisis occurred in January, when thousands of students rioted, calling for greater freedom and democracy. This brought a push by party hard-liners, firmly opposed to China's open door policy. They called for an end to Western influences and seemed to pose a threat to Mr. Deng's authority. However, the hard-liners were dealt a major blow at the Communist Party congress in November, when leaders such as President Li Xiannian and National Peoples Congress Chairman Peng Zhen were forced out to the sidelines. Mr. Deng then promoted to the Politburo young technocrats and supporters of economic reforms. Their rise to power, however, left several main problems unresolved, including inflation, which led to social unrest. Party leaders said inflation was one of the top priority issues to be settled in 1988. The open door policy in November brought the opening of China's first Western fast food restaurant, a Kentucky Fried Chicken outlet located only a stone's throw away from Mao's white marble mausoleum in Peking. But such moves revived the struggle between conservatives and reform-minded leaders, with the stakes being who will eventually take over from semi-retired Mr. Deng, who admits to working no more than two hours a day. His supporters said that the country must speed up reforms to boost an economy paralyzed by 30 years of autocracy. To conservatives, this policy smacked of capitalism. Another major clash between the two factions came in October, when pro-independence demonstrations erupted into violence in Tibet. The ten-day long anti-Chinese protests in Lhasa brought a show of force from Chinese authorities in Tibet and at least 13 people were killed. The protests put pro-reform supporters on the spot, as conservatives argued that the demonstrations resulted from overly liberal policies. In the crackdown, Tibet was virtually closed to foreigners and Western journalists were expelled. This showed that the open door policy had its limits. In November, the nomination of Li Peng, 59, as interim premier to replace Zhao Ziyang, was seen as another political compromise. As prime minister, the conservative, Soviet-trained Mr. Li is in charge of the economy. He advocated a more centrally planned economy than the liberal one pushed by Mr. Deng and his reformist supporters. His nomination was interpreted as a move to appease hard-liners, while leaving Mr. Deng in overall control of the country's affairs. In May, a huge, month-long forest fire, China's worst in 40 years, ravaged Heilongjiang province. The blaze killed over 190 people, injured 226, left 50,000 homeless and scorched two million acres. Twenty three-people were later arrested, and six forestry workers were accused of directly causing the fire.

Colombia

South America
439,735 sq. mi.
Pop. : 27,900,000
UN, LAIA,
OAS

Capital : Bogota
(Pop. : 5,000,000)
Official language : Spanish
Religion : Roman Catholic 97 %
Political status : Presidential republic
Head of state : Virgilio Barco Vargas
(since 1986)
Head of government : Virgilio Barco
Vargas
GNP : $38.8 bil. (1983)
Currency : Peso ($ 1 US = 259.58)

Political violence continued to exact
a heavy toll, with scores of civilians
caught in the crossfire between war-
ring factions. Many killings were attributed to right-wing death squads,
bringing retaliation from leftist M-19
guerrillas. A deadly September muds-
lide killed some 500 people near
Medellin. Colombia's powerful drug
lords threatened to unleash a full-
scale war in November if one of their
leaders was extradited to the U.S.

Comoros

Indian Ocean
838 sq. mi.
Pop. : 415,000
UN, OAU

Capital : Moroni (Pop. : 25,000)
Official language : French
Religions : Islam (official), Roman
Catholic
Political status : Federal Islamic republic
Head of state : Ahmed Abdallah
Abderemane (since 1978)
Head of government : Ahmed Abdallah
Abderemane
GNP : $180 mil. (1984)
Currency : CFA franc
($ 1 US = 282.55)

Congo

Central Africa
132,046 sq. mi.
Pop. : 1,980,000
UN, OAU

Capital : Brazzaville
(Pop. : 600,000)
Official language : French
Religions : Christian 50 %, animist 47 %,
Moslem 2 %
Political status : People's republic
Head of state : Denis Sassou-Nguesso
(since 1979)
Head of government : Ange Edouard
Poungui (since 1984)

GNP : $2.1 bil. (1983)
Currency : CFA franc
($ 1 US = 282.55)

Costa Rica

Central America
19,575 sq. mi.
Pop. : 2,655,000
UN, Caricom,
OAS

Capital : San Jose (Pop. : 241,000)
Official language : *Spanish*
Religion : Roman Catholic
Political status : Democratic republic
Head of state : Oscar Arias Sanchez (since
1986)
Head of government : Oscar Arias Sanchez
(since 1986)
GNP : $3.2 bil. (1984)
Currency : Colon ($ 1 US = 66.75)

After barely a year in office, President
Arias was in October awarded the
1987 Nobel Peace Prize for launching
a Central American peace plan aimed
at ending wars in Nicaragua and El
Salvador and restoring Western-style
democracy to the region. Mr. Arias
called on Nicaraguan leaders to begin
talks with the U.S.-backed contra
forces, after the presidents of El Salvador and Guatemala agreed to meet
with rebels. Despite these efforts,
peace in the region remained a distant
goal as the bloodshed continued. Colombian drug gangs moved into Costa
Rica in 1987, prompting some citizens
and politicians to hire bodyguards.

Cuba

Caribbean
44,218 sq. mi.
Pop. : 10,150,000
UN, CMEA,
OAS

Capital : Havana (Pop. : 2,000,000)
Official language : Spanish
Religions : Roman Catholic 42 %, none
49 %
Political status : Socialist republic
Head of state : Fidel Castro Ruz (since
1959)
Head of government : Fidel Castro Ruz
(since 1959)
GNP : $15.8 bil. (1983)
Currency : Cuban peso ($ 1 US = 0.73)

Twenty-five years after the Cuban
missile crisis, strained U.S.-Cuban
relations took a turn for the worse in
July, as the government accused
89 Havana-based U.S. diplomats of
being CIA agents. This followed the
embarrassing defection, to the U.S. of
a senior Cuban air force general, a
move seen as an intelligence coup for
Washington. President Castro stepped up his propaganda drive against
the CIA in a bid to mobilize public
opinion behind his efforts to face

Cuba's dire economic problems.
Cuba, criticized by the U.N. human
rights body, sought to improve the
country's image by freeing some political prisoners, allowing foreign reporters to visit local jails and refor-
ming the penal code. In November,
the London-based human rights
group Amnesty International said
there were 4,000 to 5,000 political
prisoners in Cuba. Despite pressure
from Washington, Havana continued
to support the Sandinistas in Nicaragua, kept some 37,000 soldiers in
Angola and others in Ethiopia. In
November, Cuba agreed to take back
thousands of Cubans held in U.S.
jails, sparking bloody riots by reluctant inmates in Louisiana and Georgia prisons. The prisoners came to the
U.S. in the 1980 Mariel boatlift.

Cyprus

Southern Europe
3,572 sq. mi.
Pop. : 680,000
UN, CW, EC

Capital : Nicosia (Pop. : 122,000)
Official languages : Greek, Turkish
Religions : Orthodox 77 %, Moslem 18 %
Political status : Republic
Head of state : Spyros Kyprianou (since
1977)
Head of government : Spyros Kyprianou
(since 1977)
GNP : $2.06 bil. (1984)
Currency : Cyprus pound ($ 1 US = 2.18)

This year marked the 13th anniversary of the arrival of Turkish troops,
and in July President Kyprianou called for more international pressure on
Ankara to withdraw its forces from
the northern part of the island.

Czechoslovakia

Central Europe
49,365 sq. mi.
Pop. : 15,479,642
UN, CMEA,
Warsaw Pact

Capital : Prague (Pop. : 1,250,000)
Official languages : Czech, Slovak
Religion : Roman Catholic
Political status : Federal Socialist republic
Head of state : Gustav Husak (since 1975)
Head of government : Lubomir Strougal
(since 1970)
GNP : $118.4 bil. (1984)
Currency : Czech koruna
($ 1 US = 5.40)

In a major December upheaval, Gustav Husak was replaced as leader of
the country's Communist Party by
Milos Jakes. Mr Husak, in office
since 1969, remained head of state
and kept his party Praesidium seat.

Denmark

North Europe
16,633 sq. mi.
Pop. : 5,116,273
UN, EFTA, EEC,
EC, NATO, NC,
OECD

Capital : Copenhagen (Pop. : 473,000)
Official language : Danish
Religion : Lutheran 97 %
Political status : Constitutional monarchy
Head of state : Queen Margrethe II (since
1972)
Head of government : Poul Schluter (since
1982)
GNP : $80.4 bil. (1986)
Currency : Krone ($ 1 US = 6.41)

Djibouti

Northeastern
Africa
8,494 sq. mi.
Pop. : 297,000
UN, AL, OAU

Capital : Djibouti (Pop. : 200,000)
Official languages : French, Arabic
Religion : Sunni Moslem 94 %
Political status : Presidential republic
Head of state : Hassan Gouled Aptidon
(since 1977)
Head of government : Barkat Gourad
Hamadou (since 1978)
GNP : $340 mil. (1984)
Currency : Djibouti franc
($ 1 US = 176.83)

Dominica

Caribbean
290 sq. mi.
Pop. : 74,851
UN, Caricom,
OAS

Capital : Roseau (Pop. : 20,000)
Official language : English
Religion : mainly Roman Catholic
Political status : Republic
Head of state : Clarence A. Seignoret
(since 1983)
Head of government : Mary Eugenia
Charles (since 1980)
GNP : $80 mil. (1983)
Currency : East Caribbean dollar
($ 1 US = 2.70)

Dominican Republic

Caribbean
18,816 sq. mi.
Pop. : 6,588,000
UN, OAS

Capital : Santo Domingo
(Pop. : 1,500,000)
Official language : Spanish
Religion : Roman Catholic 98 %
Political status : Presidential republic
Head of state : Joaquin Belaguer (since 1986)
Head of government : Joaquin Belaguer
GNP : $5.5 bil. (1986)
Currency : Peso ($ 1 US = 4.53)

Tensions rose with neighboring Haiti over the presence of some 500,000 Haitian immigrants. Former President Salvador Blanco was jailed in October over shady deals.

Ecuador

South America
109,483 sq. mi.
Pop. : 9,370,000
UN, LAIA, OAS

Capital : Quito (Pop. : 1,000,000)
Official language : Spanish
Religion : Roman Catholic
Political status : Presidential republic
Head of state : Leon Febres Cordero (since 1984)
Head of government : L.F. Cordero
GNP : $9.7 bil. (1985)
Currency : Sucre ($ 1 US = 290.50)

A March earthquake killed over 1,000. In January, the president was seized by rebel troops, but later freed. In July the congress demanded that U.S. troops building a road leave.

Egypt

North Africa
386,650 sq. mi.
Pop. : 48,850,000
UN, AL, OAU, OPEC

Capital : Cairo (Pop. : 5,800,000)
Official language : Arabic
Religion : Sunni Moslem 90 %
Political status : Presidential republic
Head of state : Hosni Mubarak (since 1981)
Head of government : Atef Sedki (since 1986)
GNP : $34 bil. (1985)
Currency : Egyptian pound ($ 1 US = 0.70)

Police arrested 500 Islamic militants in June after a wave of assassination bids in Cairo that sparked fears of destabilization by Moslem fundamentalists. In April, the PLO offices in Cairo were closed after the Palestinian group had called on Egypt to back away from the 1978 Camp David accords. In November, officials said the offices might be allowed to reopen. This came after more than 15 Arab states, which had broken links with Cairo after the 1979 Egyptian-Israeli peace treaty, resumed ties with Egypt. In September, Africa's first subway system opened in Cairo at a cost of some $230 million.

El Salvador

Central America
8,260 sq. mi.
Pop. : 5,480,000
UN, OAS, LAES

Capital : San Salvador
Official language : Spanish
Religion : Roman Catholic
Political status : Presidential republic
Head of state : Jose Napoleon Duarte (since 1984)
Head of government : J.N. Duarte
GNP : $4 bil. (1984)
Currency : Colon ($ 1 US = 5)

Leftist guerrilla leaders returned from exile in November under the regional peace plan launched in August. They said they wanted to find a solution to El Salvador's conflict. In October, Mr. Duarte held peace talks with leftist rebels and hopes for an end to the eight-year-old civil war rose. A total of some 62,000 people, mostly non-combatants, died in the fighting between U.S.-backed Salvadoran forces and guerrillas. The economy suffered massive disruption. In November, about 430 political prisoners were freed, but the amnesty did not include those accused of the 1980 slaying of four U.S. church workers.

Equatorial Guinea

West Africa
10,832 sq. mi.
Pop. : 375,000
UN, ECOWAS, OAU

Capital : Malabo (Pop. : 33,000)
Official language : Spanish
Religions : Rom. Cath. 83 %, Prot., others
Political status : Presidential republic
Head of state : Col. Teodoro Obiang Nguema Mbasogo (since 1979)
Head of government : T.O. Nguema
GNP : $131 mil. (1984)
Currency : CFA franc ($ 1 US = 282.55)

Ethiopia

Northeastern Africa
471,776 sq. mi.
Pop. : 42,019,418
UN, OAU

Capital : Addis Abada (Pop. : 1,500,000)
Official languages : Amharic, Galla
Religions : Orthodox Christian 40 %, Moslem 40 %
Political status : People's democratic republic
Head of state : Mengistu Haile Mariam (since 1977)
Head of government : Mengistu Haile Mariam (since 1977)
GNP : $4.6 bil. (1986)
Currency : Birr ($ 1 US = 2.07)

Lieutenant Colonel Mengistu, Ethiopia's undisputed ruler for the past ten years, was unanimously elected in September to be the first president of the newly created " People's Democratic Republic, " marking a return to civilian rule. A new republican constitution was adopted by referendum in February in a bid to turn the centuries-old feudal state into a republic. Despite the changes, famine continued to stalk the land and the regime's vow to achieve food self-sufficiency by 1990 appeared unattainable. The U.N. predicted new shortages through 1988 and called for urgent international aid. Over five million Ethiopians were threatened with starvation in 1988, as fighting continued in the rebellious Eritrean province.

Fiji

South Pacific
7,056 sq. mi.
Pop. : 714,000
UN, CW

Capital : Suva (Pop. : 80,000)
Official language : English
Religions : Christian 49 %, Hindu 40 %
Political status : Republic
Head of state : Ratu Sir Penaia Ganilau (since 12/5/87)
Head of government : Ratu Sir Kamisese Mara (since 12/5/87)
GNP : $1.18 bil. (1984)
Currency : Fiji dollar ($ 1 US = 1.50)

After a bloodless September coup, Fiji was expelled from the Commonwealth and in December former Governor General Ratu Sir Penaia Ganilau was appointed as the new republic's first president. Queen Elizabeth II thus ceased to be Fiji's head of state. Former prime minister Ratu Sir Kamisese Mara was appointed premier. The upheaval came after April elections gave power to an Indian-dominated government, a move deemed intolerable by the archipelagos' indigenous Fijians. The new president promised a return to civilian rule.

Finland

Northern Europe
130,119 sq. mi.
Pop. : 4,910,000
UN, NC, OECD

Capital : Helsinki (Pop. : 486,000)
Official languages : Finnish, Swedish
Religion : Lutheran 90 %
Political status : Democratic parliamentary republic
Head of state : Mauno Koivisto (since 1982)
Head of government : Harri Holreki (since 1987)
GNP : $70.5 bil. (1986)
Currency : Finnmark ($ 1 US = 4.08)

France

Western Europe
221,207 sq. mi.
Pop. : 55,500,000
UN, EEC, EC, OECD, NATO

Capital : Paris (Pop. : 2,900,000)
Official language : French
Religion : Mostly Roman Catholic
Political status : Democratic parliamentary republic
Head of state : François Mitterrand (since 1981)
Head of government : Jacques Chirac (since 1986)
GNP : $705.5 bil. (1986)
Currency : French franc ($ 1 US = 5.65)

Terrorism was a major yearlong issue, with a spate of bombings and killings by left-wing extremists, Corsican independence groups and Basque separatists. Police in February arrested four top leaders of the Direct Action leftist terrorist gang, while in November its last-known leader was nabbed. Mideast-related terrorism caused a five-month crisis with Iran, after an Iranian Embassy official in Paris, suspected of involvement in bloody 1986 bombings, was forbidden to leave, sparking retaliation by Tehran. The crisis was resolved in December, amid reports that Paris had agreed to supply arms to Iran in exchange for the release of French hostages held in Lebanon. In July, former Gestapo chief in Lyons Klaus Barbie was given a life sentence. Political life, shaken by several scandals, heated up ahead of the spring 1988 presidential vote.

Gabon

Central Africa
103,346 sq. mi.
Pop. : 1,336,000
UN, OAU, OPEC

Capital : Libreville (Pop. : 350,000)
Official language : French
Religions : Tribal beliefs, Christ. minority
Political status : Presidential republic
Head of state : Omar Bongo (since 1967)
Head of government : L. Mebiame (s. 75)
GNP : $2.8 bil. (1985)
Currency : CFA franc ($ 1 US = 282.55)

Gambia

West Africa
4,361 sq. mi.
Pop. : 751,000
UN, OAU, CW

Capital : Banjul (Pop.: 44,536)
Official language : English
Religions : Moslem 85 %, Christian 14 %
Political status : Republic
Head of state : Dawda Kairaba Jawara (since 1970)
Head of government : Dawda Kairaba Jawara (since 1962)
GNP : $200 mil. (1983)
Currency : Dalasi ($ 1 US = 7.44)

Germany (East)

Central Europe
41,768 sq. mi.
Pop.: 16,644,308
UN, CMEA,
Warsaw Pact

Capital : East Berlin (Pop.: 1,150,000)
Official language : German
Religion : Protestant 80 %
Political status : Socialist republic
Head of state : Erich Honecker (since 1976)
Head of government : Willi Stoph (since 1976)
GNP : $140 bil. (1983)
Currency : DDR mark ($ 1 US = 1.66)

A September visit to West Germany by State Council Chairman Honecker brought hopes of reduced tension between Bonn and Berlin, with some even speculating that the hated Berlin Wall would one day be torn down. But attempts to flee to the West continued to cost lives. A typically Western phenomenon, rock music, came to austere East Germany in the summer. There was a late-November crackdown on ecology and pacifist groups.

Germany (West)

Central Europe
95,975 sq. mi.
Pop.: 61,020,000
UN, EEC, EC,
NATO, OECD

Capital : Bonn (Pop.: 300,000)
Official language : German
Religions : Protestant 44 %, Roman Catholic 45 %
Political status : Federal republic
Head of state : Richard von Weizsacker (since 1984)
Head of government : Helmut Kohl (since 1982)
GNP : $611.8 bil. (1985)
Currency : Deutsche mark ($ 1 US = 1.66)

The pro-ecology group Greenpeace scored well in January elections. In a May visit, Pope John Paul II condemned Nazism, but neo-Nazis remained active. Strict anti-AIDS measures, mainly aimed at Third World immigrants, were taken in Bavaria. A June visit by President Reagan to West Berlin, as the city celebrated its 750th anniversary, was marked by protests. Mr. Reagan pledged that U.S. troops would stay in Berlin as long as necessary and challenged Moscow to tear down the Berlin Wall. Bonn reinforced its military ties with France ahead

of the withdrawal of medium-range U.S. missiles from Europe. In August, Hitler's former deputy Rudolf Hess died in jail, aged 93. Despite an historic September visit by East Germany's leader Erich Honecker, relations between the two countries remained tense.

Ghana

West Africa
92,098 sq. mi.
Pop.: 13,004,000
UN, CW,
ECOWAS,
OAU

Capital : Accra (Pop.: 859,000)
Official language : English
Religions : Christian 43 %, traditional beliefs 45 %
Political status : Republic
Head of state : Jerry John Rawlings (since 1981)
Head of government : Jerry John Rawlings (since 1981)
GNP : $4 bil. (1985)
Currency : New cedi ($ 1 US = 174)

Greece

Southeastern
Europe
51,146 sq. mi.
Pop.: 9,970,000
UN, EEC, EC,
NATO, OECD

Capital : Athens (Pop.: 3,000,000)
Official language : Greek
Religion : Greek Orthodox 97 %
Political status : Democratic parliamentary republic
Head of state : Christos Sartzetakis (since 1985)
Head of government : Andreas Papandreou (since 1981)
GNP : $39.1 bil. (1986)
Currency : Drachma ($ 1 US = 131.05)

Progress marked November U.S.-Greek talks aimed at the renewal of a 1983 accord on U.S. bases and troops. But soon after, over 100,000 anti-U.S. Greeks marched through Athens on the 14th anniversary of the revolt against the former military junta. Nine U.S. servicemen were hurt in an August car bomb attack. A July heat wave killed over 600. The socialist premier became embroiled in alleged infidelity to his American wife.

Grenada

Caribbean
133 sq. mi.
Pop.: 113,000
UN, CW,
Caricom, OAS

Capital : St. George's (Pop.: 7,500)
Official language : English
Religions : Roman Catholic 64 %, Anglican 22 %
Political status : Constitutional monarchy
Head of state : Queen Elizabeth II
Head of government : Herbert Blaize (since 1985)
GNP : $80 mil. (1985)
Currency : East Caribbean dollar ($ 1 US = 2.70)

Guatemala

Central America
42,042 sq. mi.
Pop.: 8,403,025
UN, OAS,
LAES

Capital : Guatemala City (Pop.: 1,300,000)
Official language : Spanish
Religion : Roman Catholic over 88 %
Political status : Presidential republic
Head of state : Vinicio Cerezo (since 1986)
Head of government : Vinicio Cerezo (since 1986)
GNP : $9.5 bil. (1985)
Currency : Quetzal ($ 1 US = 1)

The government and rebel leaders held their first talks since 1961 in October, bringing hope for an end to armed insurgency. In May, limited U.S. forces took part in a Guatemalan counter-insurgency operation. Along with Honduras, Nicaragua, El Salvador and Costa Rica, Guatemala signed an August plan aimed at ending strife and fostering democracy in the region. Improvement was reported in the country's human rights record. In October, the defense minister reportedly accused extreme rightists of seeking to destabilize the country's military.

Guinea

West Africa
94,964 sq. mi.
Pop.: 6,407,000
UN, ECOWAS,
OAU

Capital : Conakry (Pop.: 750,000)
Official language : French
Religions : Moslem 85 %, Christian 10 %
Political status : Presidential republic
Head of state : Lansana Conte (since 1984)
Head of government : Lansana Conte (since 1984)
GNP : $1.96 bil. (1984)
Currency : Guinea franc ($ 1 US = 340)

The government in May sentenced to death some 60 people for crimes committed during the rule of former President Ahmed Sekou Touré, whose tribal supporters threatened the country's stability.

Guinea-Bissau

West Africa
13,948 sq. mi.
Pop.: 875,000
UN, ECOWAS,
OAU

Capital : Bissau (Pop.: 110,000)
Official language : Portuguese
Religions : traditional 65 %, Moslem 30 %, Christian 4 %
Political status : Republic
Head of state : Joao Bernardo Vieira (since 1980)
Head of government : Joao Bernardo Vieira (since 1980)
GNP : $147 mil. (1985)
Currency : Guinea peso ($ 1 US = 650)

Guyana

South America
83,000 sq. mi.
Pop.: 950,000
UN, Caricom,
CW

Capital : Georgetown (Pop.: 170,000)
Official language : English
Religions : Christian 57 %, Hindu 34 %, Moslem 9 %
Political status : Presidential republic
Head of state : Hugh Desmond Hoyte (since 1985)
Head of government : Hamilton Green (since 1985)
GNP : $360 mil. (1986)
Currency : Guyana dollar ($ 1 US = 10)

Haiti

Caribbean
10,714 sq. mi.
Pop.: 5,272,000
UN, OAS,
LAES

Capital : Port-au-Prince (Pop.: 550,000)
Official language : French
Religions : Roman Catholic 80 %, Protestant 10 %, Voodoo widely practiced
Political status : Presidential republic
Head of state : Gen. Henri Namphy (since 1986)
Head of government : Gen. Henri Namphy (since 1986)
GNP : $1.91 bil. (1986)
Currency : Gourde ($ 1 US = 5)

Crucial November elections, the country's first free poll in 30 years, were suspended after vigilante attacks left some 35 dead. The violence was attributed to supporters of deposed dictator Jean-Claude Duvalier. The U.S. responded by cutting off all military and non-humanitarian aid to the Haitian junta. U.S. election observers were evacuated after U.S. journalists were wounded. Junta leader Namphy vowed to respect the democratic process, but many doubted that new elections would be held. In July, the impoverished nation was paralyzed by a general strike. In 1987, Haiti also became a major staging point for U.S.-bound cocaine and marijuana.

Honduras

Central America
43,277 sq. mi.
Pop.: 4,240,000
UN, OAS

Capital : Tegucigalpa (Pop.: 553,000)
Official language : Spanish
Religions : Roman Catholic, small Protestant minority
Political status : Presidential republic
Head of state : Jose Simeon Azcona Hoyo (since 1986)
Head of government : Jose Simeon Azcona Hoyo (since 1986)
GNP : $3.1 bil. (1985)
Currency : Lempira ($ 1 US = 2)

Tensions arose in eastern sectors, where local peasants, U.S.-backed contra rebels and Nicaraguan refugees cohabited uneasily. There were protests against plans to set up a contra base, as Nicaraguan forces carried out cross-border raids into southern regions. U.S. and Honduran forces held joint exercises in August. The armed forces chief charged local politicians with involvement in international drug trafficking.

Hungary

Central Europe
35,919 sq. mi.
Pop.: 10,640,000
UN, CMEA,
Warsaw Pact

Capital : Budapest (Pop.: 2,100,000)
Official language : Hungarian
Religions : Roman Catholic 67 %, Protestant 25 %
Political status : Socialist people's republic
Head of state : Karoly Nemeth (s.6/25/87)
Head of government : Karoly Grosz (since 6/25/87)
GNP : $19.66 bil. (1984)
Currency : Forint ($ 1 US = 47.79)

Iceland

North Atlantic
39,769 sq. mi.
Pop.: 242,089
UN, OECD,
NATO, NC, EC

Capital : Reykjavik (Pop.: 89,868)
Official language : Icelandic
Religion : Evangelical Lutheran 97 %
Political status : Parliamentary republic
Head of state : Vigdis Finnbogadottir (since 1980)
Head of government : Thorsteinn Palsson (since 7/9/87)
GNP : $3.6 bil. (1985)
Currency : Krona ($ 1 US = 36.86)

India

Southern Asia
1,266,595 sq. mi.
Pop.:
767,681,000
UN, CW

Capital : New Delhi (Pop.: 6,200,000)
Official languages : Hindi, English
Religions : Hindu 83 %, Moslem 11 %, Christian 3 %, Sikh 2 %
Political status : Federal parliamentary republic
Head of state : Ramaswami Venkataraman (since July 1987)
Head of government : Rajiv Gandhi (since 1984)
GNP : $160 bil. (1985)
Currency : Indian rupee ($ 1 US = 12.97)

Premier Gandhi was rocked by political opposition and renewed Gurkha, Hindu, Moslem and Sikh separatist violence. He also faced charges of political corruption. Border tensions with Pakistan rose. As India celebrated 40 years of independence, thousands of Indian peacekeeping troops fought bloody battles with Tamil separatists in Sri Lanka. India and the U.S. company Union Carbide failed to agree on damages to victims of the 1984 Bhopal gas disaster. In December, India announced plans to build the world's largest radio telescope at a cost of $16 million.

Indonesia

Southeast Asia
735,268 sq. mi.
Pop.:
163,000,000
UN, ASEAN,
OPEC

Capital : Jakarta (Pop.: 6,900,000)
Official language : Indonesian
Religion : Moslem 90 %
Political status : Presidential republic
Head of state : Gen. Kemusu Suharto (since 1967)
Head of government : Gen. Kemusu Suharto
GNP : $74.29 bil. (1985)
Currency : Rupiah ($ 1 US = 1650)

The ruling Golkar party, which won every election since General Suharto came to power 20 years ago, achieved an April landslide. In October the government chose NASA to launch its next satellite, rejecting Soviet and Chinese offers.

Iran

Middle East
636,293 sq. mi.
Pop.: 45,190,000
UN, OPEC

Capital : Tehran (Pop.: 5,700,000)
Official language : Persian
Religion : Shi'a Moslem 93 %
Political status : Islamic republic
Head of state : Sayed Ali Khamenei (since 1981)
Head of government : Hosein Musavi Khamenei (since 1981)
GNP : $132 bil. (1985)
Currency : Rial ($ 1 US = 67.98)

As 1987 drew to a close, there were persistent reports that Iran's spiritual guide, Ayatollah Khomeini, was seriously ill. The Iranian leader is aged between 85 and 87. Reliable sources said he suffered from heart and respiratory problems. In December, Khomeini changed his " political will, " a move that could weaken the position of his designated successor, Ayatollah Hussein Ali Montazeri, aged 65. The Iranian spiritual guide submitted the revised testament to the country's main leaders, to remain sealed until his death. Ayatollah Montazeri's position suffered a severe setback with the arrest and execution of several of his closest aides, notably Mehdi Hashemi, executed after being accused of plotting against the Islamic Republic. There were also reports in December that Iran's Communist Party, Tudeh, broken up in 1983, had clandestinely regrouped inside the country. The party called for a cease-fire in the Iran-Iraq war ahead of a political settlement to the bloody seven-year conflict. Tehran repeatedly vowed to continue fighting until it " crushed " Iraq, and rejected a U.N. cease-fire call, saying the United Nations must first condemn Iraq's " aggression. " The Irangate scandal revelations in Washington caused some embarrassment in Tehran, as leaders sought to deny there had been any dealing with Iran's " arch-enemy, " the U.S. Iranian authorities named November 4 " Death to America Day, " to mark the anniversary of the 1979 occupation of the U.S. Embassy in Tehran. In February, Iran arrested and later expelled Gerald Seib, a reporter for the Wall Street Journal, detained as a " spy for the Zionist regime. " Iran's relations with Western nations remained at an all-time low, and major diplomatic crises erupted with Britain, France and Saudi Arabia. Tehran promised to seek revenge for the July death in the Saudi holy city of Mecca of some 400 Iranian pilgrims. As the crisis deepened in the Gulf and the U.S., Britain, France and others boosted their forces in the region, Tehran and Moscow in 1987 stepped up their contacts. Mines laid by Iran to disrupt shipping in the Gulf were reported to be Soviet-made. The Soviet Union also criticized the increased U.S. Navy presence in the Gulf. Iran bought and used to deadly effect Chinese-built Silkworm anti-ship

missiles, sparking U.S protests to Peking. Iranian forces began in mid-summer to use gun-bearing speedboats against commercial vessels in the Gulf. The craft were highly mobile, but avoided direct confrontation with U.S. forces on patrol in the Gulf, striking instead at vulnerable oil tankers. Despite calls for arms embargoes, clandestine weapons shipments continued to prop up Iran's war machinery. Iranian forces also suffered huge losses in " human wave " attacks against Iraqi-held positions, but succeeded in retaking territory on the southern front. Some 150,000 Iranian schoolboys were reported to be at the war front. The Iranian regime continued to support Islamic revolutionary groups abroad, including Lebanon's Hezbollah cells, said to be directly linked to the capture and detention of Western hostages.

Iraq

Middle East
167,924 sq. mi.
Pop.: 15,400,000
UN, AL, OPEC

Capital : Baghdad (Pop.: 3,500,000)
Official language : Arabic
Religions : Moslem 95 % (Shiite 55 %, Sunni 40 %), Christian 5 %
Political status : Socialist presidential republic
Head of state : Saddam Hussein (since 1979)
Head of government : Saddam Hussein (since 1979)
GNP : $29.7 bil. (1984)
Currency : Dinar ($ 1 US = 0.31)

Baghdad suffered a stinging international setback in May when an Iraqi warplane fired a French-made Exocet missile at the U.S. frigate Stark, killing 37 crew members. The Stark was on patrol in international waters in the Gulf. President Hussein termed the blunder an " unintentional accident " and launched an internal inquiry, and President Reagan said he accepted the Iraqi explanation. The bitter seven-year war with Iran raged on, and in January Tehran launched a major month-long offensive along the southern front, claiming to have retaken large parts of Iraqi-held territory. Iraqi aircraft repeatedly raided Iranian oil facilities near Tabriz, Tehran and at the Kharg terminal. Iraqi planes also bombed industrial and civilian targets in Iran, and Tehran responded with missile attacks on Baghdad, where in October a missile landed on a school, killing some 30 children. Since the start of the war, Iraq has lost over 60 warplanes, or ten percent of its air force, but the Soviet Union agreed to replace the losses. In 1987, Iraq was reported to have replaced Saudi Arabia as the world's biggest arms buyer, purchasing mostly Soviet and French materiel. Baghdad however, denied using chemical weapons against Iranian troops. The war and falling oil prices caused major economic problems. Iraqi forces also suffered losses in battles with Kurdish guerrillas fighting for autonomy in the north and east. Turkey and Iraq stepped up joint anti-guerrilla operations along the border in a bid to crush the Kurds' rebellion.

Ireland

Western Europe
27,137 sq. mi.
Pop. : 3,537,195
UN, EEC, EC,
OECD

Capital : Dublin (Pop. : 920,000)
Official languages : Irish (Gaelic), English
Religions : Roman Catholic 94 %,
Anglican 4 %
Political status : Parliamentary republic
Head of state : Patrick J.Hillery (since 1976)
Head of government : Charles J.Haughey (since Feb. 1987)
GNP :$25.1 bil. (1986)
Currency : Irish pound ($ 1 US = 1.59)

After a close March vote, Charles Haughey of the Fianna Fail party was elected prime minister for the third time, succeeding Garret FitzGerald, whose governing coalition collapsed in January. The new premier's first task was to put the economy back on track. At over $33 billion, Ireland's foreign debt is one of the largest among industrialized nations. In May, voters lifted the final obstacle to a treaty boosting cooperation among EEC countries. The 1985 signing of the Anglo-Irish agreement, which gives Dublin a say in Northern Ireland's affairs, came under renewed Protestant attack in Ulster. In November, Dublin said it would apply a European anti-terrorism convention containing key provisions for the extradition of terrorist suspects. However, Eire in December hinted it may delay implementation of the convention.

Israel

Near East
7,847 sq. mi.
Pop. : 4,233,000
UN

Capital : Jerusalem (Pop. : 465,000)
Official language : Hebrew
Religions : Jewish 83 %, Moslem 13 %
Political status : Parliamentary republic
Head of state : Chaim Herzog (since 1983)
Head of government : Yitzhak Shamir (since 1986)
GNP : $20 bil. (1986)
Currency : New shekel ($ 1 US = 1.57)

The year brought no major breakthrough in the search for peace between Israel and its Arab neighbors, despite some glimmers of hope. The idea of an international Mideast peace conference was placed indefinitely on hold after Israeli objections to allowing the Soviet Union to play a major role in any peace talks. 1987 was marked by a long-running quarrel over the issue between Mr. Shamir, leader of the conservative Likud bloc, and Foreign Minister Shimon Peres of the Labor Party. The premier firmly rejected the international framework, while Mr. Peres favored the plan. Despite U.S. pressure, Mr. Shamir stood firm. In a bid to break the stalemate, Washington in October proposed a new peace framework entailing direct Israeli-Jordanian talks, under the umbrella of an international group, with limited Soviet representation. The question remained whether Moscow would accept a reduced role. Mr. Shamir said he would only agree to discuss Mideast peace with the Soviets if the Kremlin allowed the free emigration of Soviet Jews and resumed relations with Israel. In July, a Soviet delegation made the first official visit to Israel since ties were broken after the 1967 Mideast war. However, the visit did not lead to a breakthrough. In February, Soviet Jewish dissident Anatoly Shcharansky, released by the Kremlin, arrived to a hero's welcome in Jerusalem. Ira Nudel, dubbed the " guardian angel " of refuseniks, arrived in Israel after a 16-year battle to leave the Soviet Union. Two major trials opened in 1987. John Demjanjuk appeared in the dock charged with Nazi war crimes. Nuclear technician Mordechai Vanunu was accused of leaking details of Israel's nuclear program. In September, the government decided to scrap the Lavi fighter plane project after heated debate. Six Israeli soldiers died in a November hangglider suicide attack on an army camp by Palestinian commandos. Violent clashes marred the summer as Orthodox Jews protested in Jerusalem against showing movies on the Sabbath. At the year's end, the worst Arab rioting in 20 years occured on the Gaza strip and West Bank.

Italy

Southern Europe
116,303 sq. mi.
Pop. : 57,202,000
UN, EEC, EC,
NATO, OECD

Capital : Rome (Pop. : 3,000,000)
Official language : Italian
Religion : Roman Catholic
Political status : Parliamentary republic
Head of state : Francesco Cossiga (since 1985)
Head of government : Giovanni Goria (since 7/27/87)
GNP : $354 bil. (1985)
Currency : Lira ($ 1 US = 1,225)

Political crises continued to shake the country, as coalition governments came to power only to fall weeks or months later, notably over party infighting and economic policy. The country's 46th government since World War II fell in November, but the coalition was reconstituted as the nation was paralyzed by a general strike. In a referendum, a majority voted for a stop to nuclear power station building. A former porn star was elected to Parliament.

Ivory Coast

West Africa
124,503 sq. mi.
Pop. : 10,595,000
UN, ECOWAS,
OAU

Capital : Abidjan (Pop. : 1,900,000)
Official language : French
Religions : Moslem 15 %, Christian 12 %, indigenous 63 %
Political status : Presidential republic
Head of state : Felix Houphouet-Boigny (since 1960)
Head of government : Felix Houphouet-Boigny (since 1960)
GNP : $6.4 bil. (1985)
Currency : CFA franc ($ 1 US = 282.55)

Jamaica

Caribbean
4,232 sq. mi.
Pop. : 2,360,000
UN, OAS,
Caricom, CW

Capital : Kingston (Pop. : 565,800)
Official language : English
Religion : Protestant 70 %
Political status : Constitutional monarchy
Head of state : Queen Elizabeth II
Head of government : Edward P. Seaga (since 1980)
GNP : $1.7 bil. (1985)
Currency : Jamaican dollar ($ 1 US = 5.43)

After five years of stagnation, the economy spurted ahead due to improved mining and tourism. The September murder of reggae star Peter Tosh turned into a national soap opera.

Japan

Northwestern
Pacific Ocean
145,856 sq. mi.
Pop. :
121,047,000
UN, OECD

Capital : Tokyo (Pop. : 8,400,000)
Official language : Japanese
Religions : Buddhism, Shintoism
Political status : Parliamentary monarchy
Head of state : Emperor Hirohito (since 1926)
Head of government : Noboru Takeshita (since 11/6/87)
GNP : $1,958.5 bil. (1986)
Currency : Yen ($ 1 US = 134.45)

Noboru Takeshita was in November elected Japan's 46th prime minister. He inherited a slew of economic problems from his predecessor, Yasuhiro Nakasone. The election came amid widespread turmoil on stock and foreign exchange markets and continuing trade frictions with the U.S. and Western European nations. He called on Japan to make sacrifices to reduce exports and open its markets to foreign competition, saying that top priority would be given to improving relations with Washington. The new premier was due to make his first official visit to the U.S. in early 1988. The Reagan administration and Congress in 1987 moved closer to systematic economic reprisals against Japan, which continued to have a massive trade surplus with the U.S. In a December move seen as a bid to reduce U.S. resentment, Japan allocated $20 million to help peace efforts in the Gulf war. Tokyo, which gets 55 percent of its oil from the Gulf, also proposed to set up a $10 million navigation aid system to ensure the safety of shipping in the strife-torn Gulf. In another conciliatory move, Japan dropped plans to develop a new generation of fighter aircraft on its own, opting to work with the U.S. on the project. The plane, code-named FSX, is to become operational in the 1990's. The 1987 surge of the yen and the emergence of Japan as a financial superpower forced Tokyo to consider letting its currency play a wider global role. The Japanese currency continued its steady rise against the greenback. Japanese officials said the dollar could no longer fulfill its role as the world's main reserve currency because the U.S. had become the planet's most indebted nation. In the summer, Japan was rocked by a scandal over illegal sales of sophisticated Western technology to the Soviet Union. Toshiba Machine Co.'s export of milling machines boosted the Soviet Union's propeller production capability and made Soviet submarines much harder to detect. The sales caused further tensions between Washington and Tokyo. Japan announced tighter control on exports to the Soviet Union after the scandal, but this did not put a dent in the anti-Japanese mood on Capitol Hill. In July, Tokyo's high court confirmed a four-year jail term imposed on former Premier Kakuei Tanaka for accepting over $3 million in bribes in the 1976 Lockheed affair. The country in August celebrated the 42nd anniversary of the end of World War II amid charges of a resurgence of militarism. Opposition politicians denounced the buildup of Japan's Self Defense Forces and criticized the government's approval in July of Japanese participation in research for President Reagan's Strategic Defense Initiative, or " Star Wars ". There were fears in September over Emperor Hirohito's health after the 86-year-old monarch underwent an operation. The emperor, who resumed limited duties in November, is the world's oldest reigning monarch. Despite international pressure, Japan said in September that it would continue hunting whales for scientific purposes. Wildlife groups called on Mr. Reagan to impose economic sanctions on the Japanese fishing industry unless it scrapped plans to catch Minke and sperm whales. In December, a Japanese fighter fired tracer rounds as it intercepted a Soviet bomber that had intruded into Japan's airspace near a major U.S. military base on Okinawa. It was the first time a Japanese warplane had fired a warning burst at a Soviet aircraft violating Japan's airspace. Moscow later apologized.

Jordan

Middle East
37,737 sq. mi.
Pop. : 3,500,000
UN, AL

Capital : Amman (Pop. : 1,100,000)
Official language : Arabic
Religions : Sunni Moslem 94 %, Christian 5 %
Political status : Constitutional monarchy
Head of state : King Hussein II (since 1952)
Head of government : Zaid al-Rifai (since 1985)
GNP : $4,7 bil. (1986)
Currency : Dinar ($ 1 US = 0.346)

King Hussein brought together Arab rivals for a landmark November Arab League summit focused on the Gulf war and Mideast peace. After a three-year break, Jordan restored ties with Libya in September. Amman sought backing for an international Mideast peace conference, despite strong Israeli opposition and U.S. reluctance to give Moscow a major say in the region's affairs.

Kenya

Eastern Africa
224,960 sq. mi.
Pop. : 20,330,000
UN, CW, OAU

Capital : Nairobi (Pop. : 1,500,000)
Official language : Swahili
Religions : Protestant 38 %, Roman Catholic 28 %, Moslem 6 %, others
Political status : Presidential republic
Head of state : Daniel arap Moi (since 1978)
Head of government : Daniel arap Moi (since 1978)
GNP : $5.75 bil. (1984)
Currency : Kenya shilling ($ 1 US = 16.69)

Kiribati

Pacific
335 sq. mi.
Pop. : 62,000
CW

Capital : Tarawa (Pop. : 22,148)
Official language : English
Religions : Protestant, Roman Catholic
Political status : Presidential republic
Head of state : Ieremia Tabai (since 1979)
Head of government : Ieremia Tabai (since 1979)
GNP : $30 mil. (1983)
Currency : Australian dollar ($ 1 US = 1.44)

Korea (North)

Northeastern Asia
46,540 sq. mi.
Pop. : 20,550,000

Capital : Pyongyang (Pop. : 1,500,000)
Official language : Korean
Religions : Buddhism, Confucianism, Chondokyo
Political status : Democratic people's republic
Head of state : Kim Il Sung (since 1972)
Head of government : Li Gun Mo (since 1986)
GNP : $34 bil. (1984)
Currency : Won ($ 1 US = 0.94)

In July, North Korea said it would cut its army by 100,000 men in a bid to slash military spending as the country tried to bolster its economy. Pyongyang said both North and South Korea should reduce their forces to 100,000 troops each by 1992 and called for a pullout of U.S. forces from the South. But Washington said there was no way to verify Pyongyang's troop-cut claims. In May, at least ten people were reported killed when police opened fire on demonstrators in the capital.

Korea (South)

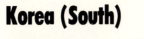

Northeastern Asia
38,025 sq. mi.
Pop. : 41,400,000

Capital : Seoul (Pop. : 9,600,000)
Official language : Korean
Religions : Buddhism, Confucianism, Christianity
Political status : Presidential republic
Head of state : Chun Doo Hwan (since 1980)
Head of government : Kim Chong Yul (since July 1987)
GNP : $87.5 bil. (1986)
Currency : Won ($ 1 US = 797.30)

The ruling party's candidate, Roh Tae Woo won December presidential elections, but opposition leaders said there had been massive fraud at the polls. It was the first direct presidential election in 16 years. Mr. Roh, who was to take office formally in February 1988 when outgoing president Chun Doo Hwan steps down, denied any wrongdoing by his camp. Mr. Roh was President Chun's hand-picked successor. Many attributed the opposition's poor showing to a lack of a single opposition candidate, adding that if the anti-Roh forces had merged they could have easily beaten the ruling Democratic Justice Party. The two main opposition leaders, Kim Dae Jung and Kim Young Sam, in fact won between them over 52 percent of votes, against Mr. Roh's 36 percent. They later apologized to opposition supporters for the lack of unity that led to their joint defeat. The ruling candidate's win sparked protests in Seoul, while U.S. election observers said they had witnessed irregularities and attacks on individuals during the election. News of Mr. Roh's win brought a surge in the South Korean stock market. In Washington, U.S. officials said the new Seoul government must liberalize its restrictive trade practices and honor past promises to allow U.S. firms greater room to operate on the South Korean market. The country's economy continued to boom, with an annual growth rate of some 13 percent. Seoul said it hoped to reduce the foreign debt to $35 billion by the end of 1987, from a peak of $47 billion in 1986. The elections followed a long, bitterly contested campaign. After over two weeks of nationwide rioting, the government in June unveiled a sweeping package of democratic reforms. During the rioting, a student protester was killed, over 13,000 demonstrators rounded up and 5,500 policemen injured. The authorities in July released some 2,000 political prisoners. The introduction of democratic reforms came after strong pressure from Washington, which urged compromise and publicly warned the government against a military solution to the crisis. The U.S. maintains about 40,000 troops in South Korea, mostly deployed along the heavily guarded 38th parallel that separates North and South Korea. A senior U.S. official in September said that U.S. troops would leave if a majority of South Koreans wanted them to, despite Washington's interest in maintaining a presence there. The heated presidential campaign did not slow preparations for the 1988 Seoul Olympics. They were due to be completed by May 1988. South Koreans were practically unanimous over the importance of the Games as a symbol of progress and a step toward entering the league of fully fledged industrialized nations. By the time the 24th Olympiad opens in September 1988, South Korea expected to have spent over $3 billion on the Games. However, there were fears of sabotage or an attack by Communist North Korea, and security remained tight. During the 1986 Asian Games in Seoul, five people died in a

bomb attack and South Korea said Pyongyang was responsible. North Korea threatened to organize a boycott of the Olympics by Communist nations, particularly its two main allies, China and the Soviet Union. But both Peking and Moscow seemed prepared to ignore a boycott call by North Korea. Pyongyang wanted to co-host the games and hold more events than offered by Olympic officials. Talks to settle the dispute were to be held in early 1988. Over 300 died in July when a typhoon lashed the country. In August, 32 cult followers of a 48-year-old woman, who claimed to be a living god, committed mass suicide and murder south of Seoul.

Kuwait

Middle East
6,880 sq. mi.
Pop. : 1,770,000
UN, AL, GCC, OPEC

Capital : Kuwait (Pop. : 60,500)
Official language : Arabic
Religion : Islam 85 %
Political status : Emirate
Head of state : Shaikh Jabir al-Ahmad al-Sabah (since 1978)
Head of government : Shaikh Saad Abdulla al-Salim al-Sabah (since 1978)
GNP : $20.5 bil. (1986)
Currency : Dinar ($ 1 US = 0.27)

Kuwait became embroiled in the Gulf war, with several bomb attacks in the capital and Iranian missiles hitting port facilities. After repeated Iranian attacks on Kuwaiti shipping in the Gulf, the country placed 11 of its tankers under U.S. Navy protection by re-flagging them. Despite increased U.S. protection, Kuwaiti ships were damaged by Iranian-laid mines and rocket attacks. Five Iranian diplomats were expelled in September. Kuwait ignored threats from Tehran and refused to free 17 pro-Iranian Moslem fundamentalists jailed for a 1983 wave of car bomb attacks.

Laos

Southeast Asia
91,428 sq. mi.
Pop. : 3,670,000
UN, CMEA

Capital : Vientiane (Pop. : 300,000)
Official language : Lao
Religions : Buddhists 58 %, tribal 34 %
Political status : Democratic people's rep.
Head of state : Poumi Vongvichit
Head of government : Kaysone Phomvihan (since 1975)
GNP : 880 mil. (1984)
Currency : New kip ($ 1 US = 35)

Lebanon

Near East
4,015 sq. mi.
Pop. : 2,619,000
UN, AL

Capital : Beirut (Pop. : 900,000)
Official language : Arabic
Religions : Moslem 60 %, Maronite
Christian 25 %, Greek Orthodox 7 %,
Druze 7 %
Political status : Parliamentary republic
Head of state : Amin Pierre Gemayel
(since 1982)
Head of government : Selim Hoss (since
6/2/87)
GNP : $3bil. (1986)
Currency : Lebanese pound
($ 1 US = 480)

1987, marked by continued bloodletting, hostage-taking, political paralysis and economic crisis, was Lebanon's darkest year since the devastating 1914 famine. In January, four Americans were seized by gunmen, days before the Archbishop of Canterbury's special envoy to Beirut, Terry Waite, was taken hostage. By year's end, eight U.S. nationals were still being held captive. A pro-Iranian religious leader said their fate was linked to the 1988 U.S. presidential elections. American journalist Charles Glass was freed in August after two months in captivity. In September, a West German hostage was released and a month later a South Korean was freed after being held hostage for 20 months. As 1987 ended, there were still 19 foreigners, including three Britons and three Frenchmen, held hostage in Lebanon. The November release of two French hostages brought a spate of reports that Paris had won their freedom by agreeing to sell arms to Iran and cracking down on Iranian exiles in France. In a bizarre November incident, a Palestinian group claimed to have seized eight Belgian and French nationals who were on a pleasure cruise of Lebanon's coast. The group said its captives were being questioned. The country's national unity government, formed in 1984, became totally paralyzed due to factional disputes. It resigned in May and President Gemayel refused to replace it. Two major political figures died in 1987 : Premier Rashid Karami, assassinated in June, and former president Camille Chamoun, known as the "godfather" of the Christian community, who died in August, aged 87. Thousands of Palestinian refugees spent months without supplies in besieged camps near Beirut. The food blockade, imposed by anti-Palestinian militiamen, was lifted after some 10,000 Syrian troops marched into West Beirut to quell factional fighting. But Syrian forces soon became the target of sniper and bomb attacks. In September, about 40 people were killed in an Israeli air raid on a Palestinian camp near Sidon. It was the year's bloodiest Israeli attack on Palestinian camps. Israel said the raid was aimed against a base used for

launching terrorist attacks on its territory. The bloodshed and political disarray hit the frail economy hard. The U.S. dollar, worth 86 Lebanese pounds in January, was worth nearly 500 pounds at year's end, while inflation reached 650 percent. The U.N. in October said Lebanon urgently needed over $85 million to make up for some of the losses suffered during the 12-year civil war. In November, the country was paralyzed by its worst general strike since 1952.

Lesotho

Southern Africa
11,716 sq. mi.
Pop. : 1,512,000
UN, CW, OAU

Capital : Maseru (Pop. : 80,250)
Official language : Sesotho
Religions : Roman Catholic 43 %,
Protestant 49 %
Political status : Constitutional monarchy
Head of state : King Moshoeshoe II (since
1966)
Head of government : Gen. Justin
Lekhanya (since 1986)
GNP : $560 (1984)
Currency : Maloti($ 1 US = 1.96)

Liberia

West Africa
38,250 sq. mi.
Pop. : 2,250,000
UN, ECOWAS,
OAU

Capital : Monrovia (Pop. : 425,000)
Official language : English
Religions : Moslem 15 %, Christian 10 %,
traditional beliefs 65 %
Political status : Presidential republic
Head of state : Samuel Kanyon Doe (since
1980)
Head of government : Samuel Kanyon
Doe (since 1980)
GNP : $1 bil. (1984)
Currency : Liberian dollar ($ 1 US = 1)

Libya

North Africa
679,359 sq. mi.
Pop. : 3,960,000
UN, AL, OAU,
OPEC

Capital : Tripoli (Pop. : 1,000,000)
Official language : Arabic
Religion : Sunni Moslem 97 %
Political status : Socialist people's state
Head of state : Muammar al-Khadafy
(since 1970)
Head of government : M. al-Khadafy
GNP : $20 bil. (1986)
Currency : Dinar ($ 1 US = 0.28)

As Libyans celebrated the 18th anniversary of Khadafy's seizure of power, Libyan forces recaptured a strategic oasis town in neighboring Chad. This success was short-lived, and Libyan forces suffered a series of major defeats at the hands of French- and U.S.-backed Chadian troops. Western trade sanctions and the worldwide oil price slump hit the economy hard, but Tripoli was reported to be continuing its aid to terrorist and rebel groups overseas, including the IRA in Ulster. Khadafy kept up his support of Iran in the Gulf war and vowed to vanquish "U.S. imperialism." The regime claimed in September that the 1986 U.S. air raids against Tripoli and Benghazi caused some $400 million worth of damages and killed 41 people. Libya also urged Arab nations to develop the atom bomb to counter the « Zionist threat. »

Liechtenstein

Western Europe
62 sq. mi.
Pop. : 27,076
EFTA, EC

Capital : Vaduz (Pop. : 4,900)
Official language : German
Religions : Roman Catholic 82 %,
Protestant 7 %
Political status : Constitutional monarchy
Head of state : Prince Franz Josef II (since
1938)
Head of government : Hans Brunhart
(since 1978)
Currency : Swiss franc ($ 1 US = 1.36)

Luxembourg

Western Europe
998 sq. mi.
Pop. : 367,200
UN, EEC, EC,
NATO,
OECD

Capital : Luxembourg (Pop. : 81,000)
Official languages : Luxembourgian,
French, German
Religion : Roman Catholic 94 %
Political status : Constitutional monarchy
Head of state : Grand Duke Jean (s. 1964)
Head of government : Jacques Santer
(since 1984)
GNP : $5.1 bil. (1986)
Currency : Lux. franc ($ 1 US = 34.80)

Madagascar

Indian Ocean
226,657 sq. mi.
Pop. : 10,294,000
UN, OAU

Capital : Antananarivo (Pop. : 650,000)
Official languages : French, Malagasy
Religions : Christian 51 %, Moslem 2 %,
animist 47 %
Political status : Republic
Head of state : Didier Ratsiraka (since
1975)
Head of government : Col. Desire
Rakotoarijaona (since 1977)
GNP : $2.23 bil. (1984)
Currency : Malagasy franc
($ 1 US = 1263.69)

Malawi

Southern Africa
45,747 sq. mi.
Pop. : 7,500,000
UN, CW, OAU

Capital : Lilongwe (Pop. : 186,800)
Official languages : English, Chichewa
Religions : Christian 75 %, Moslem 20 %
Political status : Presidential republic
Head of state : Hastings Kamuzu Banda
(since 1966)
Head of government : Hastings Kamuzu
Banda (since 1966)
GNP : 1.4 bil. (1986)
Currency : Kwacha ($ 1 US = 2.12)

Malaysia

Southeast Asia
127,316 sq. mi.
Pop. : 16,100,000
UN, ASEAN,
CW

Capital : Kuala Lumpur (Pop. : 1,100,000)
Official language : Malay
Religions : Moslem, Hindu, Buddhist,
Confucian, Taoist, local religions
Political status : Federal constitutional
monarchy
Head of state : Sultan Mahmood Iskandar
(since 1984)
Head of government : Mohamad Mahathir
(since 1981)
GNP : $29.7 bil. (1983)
Currency : Ringgit ($ 1 US = 2.49)

Premier Mahatir won a key April re-election, then purged Cabinet dissidents who had sought his ouster. In August, the former British colony celebrated its 30th independence anniversary amid fears that tensions between the three dominant races could rise.

Maldives

Indian Ocean
115 sq. mi.
Pop. : 180,000
UN